PRAISE FOR
THE MAGIC IN THE TRAGIC

"A poignant book on compassion, finding dignity in suffering, and opening up to all of life—which means loving deeply and caring deeply, and also understanding the inevitable loss that comes with that. Tragic optimism is an essential quality to a meaningful and textured life, and this book gets to the heart of what it means and how to cultivate it."

—BRAD STULBERG, BESTSELLING AUTHOR OF *THE PRACTICE OF GROUNDEDNESS* AND *MASTER OF CHANGE*

"With abundant grace and keen insight, John Tsilimparis has written a book that demystifies grief and illuminates its superpower: cultivating resilience. *The Magic in the Tragic* weaves personal experience with cultural interpretations of loss to create a much-needed roadmap through grief. Compelling, engaging, and enlightening."

—CLAUDIA KALB, AUTHOR OF *ANDY WARHOL WAS A HOARDER* AND *SPARK*

"Drawing from a rich trove of psychology, art, music, and literature, Tsilimparis explores 'tragic optimism,' the power to find beauty in suffering, and offers tools to cultivate emotional resilience. Through real-life examples and practical advice, this book redefines grief as a transformative experience, inspiring readers to discover the unexpected light within life's darkest moments."

—ELLEN HENDRIKSEN, PhD, AUTHOR OF *HOW TO BE ENOUGH*

THE MAGIC IN THE TRAGIC

REWRITING THE SCRIPT ON GRIEF AND DISCOVERING HAPPINESS IN OUR DARKEST DAYS

JOHN TSILIMPARIS, MFT

The Magic in the Tragic

Copyright © 2025 John Tsilimparis

All rights reserved. No portion of this book may be reproduced, stored in a retrieval system, or transmitted in any form or by any means—electronic, mechanical, photocopy, recording, scanning, or other—except for brief quotations in critical reviews or articles, without the prior written permission of the publisher.

Published by Harper Celebrate, an imprint of HarperCollins Focus LLC.

Any internet addresses (websites, blogs, etc.) in this book are offered as a resource. They are not intended in any way to be or imply an endorsement by HarperCollins Focus LLC, nor does HarperCollins Focus LLC vouch for the content of these sites for the life of this book.

Note: This book is not meant to be used, nor should it be used, to diagnose or treat any medical or psychological condition. Readers are advised to consult their own medical advisers whose responsibility it is to determine the condition of, and best treatment for, the reader. This publication is meant to be a source of valuable information; however, it is not meant as a substitute for direct expert assistance. If such level of assistance is required, the services of a competent professional should be sought.

All names in patient case studies have been changed to protect their identities.

Cover design by Kathy Mitchell
Art direction by Tiffany Forrester
Interior design by Kristy Edwards
Photography by Axel Koester (page 223 and jacket)

ISBN 978-1-4002-5154-4 (HC)
ISBN 978-1-4002-5156-8 (Audio)
ISBN 978-1-4002-5155-1 (epub)

Printed in Malaysia

25 26 27 28 29 SEM 5 4 3 2 1

CONTENTS

Introduction: Finding the Magic vii

1. Discovering the Dignity in Suffering
   Seeing the Beauty Within the Beast 1

2. Reauthoring Our Wounds
   Moving from Sadness to Inspiration 17

3. Accessing Spiritual Well-Being
   The Power of Something Outside Ourselves 35

4. Healthy Aloneness
   Learning How to Ground Our Emotions 49

5. Finding the Optimism in Depression
   An Uninvited Catalyst 65

6. Why We Worry
   Seeing Anxiety as an Asset 81

7. The Myth of Closure
   Slowing Down Our Timeline on Grief 103

8. Mindfulness
   Developing an Alternative Relationship with Discomfort .. 119

9. The Power of Self-Regulation

   Deactivating the Threat Response 133

10. The Need for Nostalgia

    Looking Back to Create a More Hopeful Future 149

11. The Importance of Emotional Vulnerability

    How to Build Self-Compassion 161

12. Learning to Live Like the Ocean

    Going with the Flow 179

Final Thoughts 195

Art, Music, and Drama References 201

Notes 203

Bibliography 215

Acknowledgments 219

About the Author 223

INTRODUCTION

Finding the Magic

GRIEF IS ONE OF THE MOST UNIFYING ASPECTS OF BEING human. Eventually we will all experience death, loss, or suffering. But what if I told you that there is magic in tragedy? That it's possible to cultivate meaning and purpose, even when we are grieving? That if we understand the tragedies of life are linked with beauty, poignancy, and human connectedness, we can build emotional resilience and, ultimately, reduce our suffering?

Psychologist, author, and Holocaust survivor Viktor Frankl coined the term *tragic optimism* as the ability to sustain hopefulness despite the unavoidable trials and tribulations of being human.[1] Tragic optimism is not an optimism that just "puts on a happy face" or "smiles through the tears" as though sadness is the enemy and happiness is the goal. Rather, it's a way of seeing purpose in grief, a way of embracing our full humanity (the highs *and* lows), a way of preparing ourselves for the loss and change that will inevitably come in the future.

> BY DISCOVERING THE MAGIC IN THE TRAGIC, WE CAN APPROACH GRIEF IN A NEW WAY.

When we are at our lowest in the depths of grief, it may seem impossible to hope for this kind of optimism. But if we can accept pain as part of being human, grief as something inevitable but natural to our lives and our survival, we can get closer to hope. By building emotional resilience and discovering the magic in the tragic, we can approach grief in a new way. We don't have to fear it or avoid it.

Building emotional resilience is acknowledging that discomfort will come and embracing it when it does. In *Master of Change*, author Brad Stulberg wrote, "Individuals who face life with a mindset of tragic optimism . . . feel less pain, gain more fortitude, and are more likely to successfully move forward following disruption."[2] In other words, it's okay to prepare for hard times. It might even help you move forward. Chronically avoiding discomfort and being too attached to the ideal of always being happy can be perilous, and it's simply unrealistic. If we instead prepare for the tragedies and difficult times, we will be more emotionally stable—resilient, even.

WHAT IS EMOTIONAL RESILIENCE?

Emotional resilience is the ability to overcome misfortune and bounce back from adversity. It's when we psychologically

INTRODUCTION

find ways to manage our lives in spite of serious threats to our sense of safety and security, our personal growth, and our development. Nassir Ghaemi, author of *A First-Rate Madness*, emphatically believes that "resilience isn't simply something one is born with; it grows out of an *interaction* between factors that promote it . . . and harmful life events—producing a good outcome in the end."[3] Emotional resilience is the result of being exposed to difficulty where we have to learn healthy coping skills and acquire the ability to anticipate when difficulties will come again. Since resilience comes from experiencing life on its terms, we all have the power to acquire and grow it.

Having emotional resilience means that we are not victims of our internal or external circumstances. Instead, we are the architects of our destiny. We have the power to convert trauma, grief, hardship, and any adversity into thriving. *That* power—the mechanism of embracing the grief and seeking the magic in the tragic—gives you agency and strength. By bringing new attention to suffering in this way, you can gain a sense of personal empowerment over your thoughts and feelings that in the past you had no control over. You can take charge of your emotions and experience them on *your* terms.

Building emotional resilience takes work. American Buddhist and author Pema Chödrön proposed that it's like training to be a warrior—the peaceful kind, of course.[4] She says the goal of a warrior's education is not avoiding uncertainty and distress but knowing how to best metabolize and process it. The key to processing comes "when we sit with discomfort without trying to fix it, when we stay present to the pain of approval or betrayal and let it soften us."[5] We can alter the narrative of our pain and hold the tenderness of grief. We can learn to adapt to uncertainty and instability with a relative degree of composure.

PREPARING FOR UNCERTAINTY IN UNCERTAIN TIMES

Not only do we have personal grief and suffering to anticipate and respond to, but we also live in a volatile world full of uncertainty. As a psychotherapist for over three decades, I'm hearing new questions from clients every day. For example, *How do we stay strong in uncertain times? What if disaster strikes and I am unable to provide for my family? What kind of world are we leaving for our children?*

So much of our world is up in the air, and stress levels are sky-high right now. Whether it's work, relationships, a pandemic, a volatile economy, wars overseas, mass shootings, political divisiveness, climate change, loss, death, loneliness, Zoom fatigue, technology-induced anxiety—or a combination of all—these have added to the collective worry that overwhelms us. How do we process or, better yet, appropriately grieve something like the pandemic—four years of sickness, death, and isolation? How do we function when wars and violence break out every day? Can we cultivate emotional resilience moving forward?

INTRODUCTION

While we process the grief of the past and manage the volatile present, we can do the work now to prepare for the future. In fact, it's always easier to *prevent* a mental health condition than it is to repair one. Social critic Maggie Jackson wrote that new scientific discoveries tell us that "leaning in" to uncertainty in our lives, as opposed to running from it, promotes improved mental health. In other words, building a program of fear and uncertainty management, instead of avoidance, is the best way forward. "We should rethink our outdated notions of not knowing as weakness, and instead discover this mindset as a strength," said Jackson.[6]

We need to adapt to our uncertain times; they aren't going away. By acclimatizing to the new normal of unpredictability and rapid change, we can learn and adapt. Our flexible brains can indeed habituate to the capriciousness of life's ups and downs. But first, we must consciously surrender to the unease that will naturally follow from such a drastic and radical new path. The same goes for how we rethink our grief.

THE IMPORTANCE OF ART AND NATURE

One of the ways *The Magic in the Tragic* gets us to rethink our grief is by examining the relationship between misfortune and beauty with stories, art, poetry, philosophy, movies, musical references, and nature. The arts have a universal power to affect our emotions despite what's going on around us. For

INTRODUCTION

example, music—even the melancholy kind—has a way of validating our grief. It legitimizes our pain and allows us to feel the pain without censure. You can find the vital aesthetic in your deepest feelings and use it to your advantage.

The greatest pieces of art and music have the power to pull equally from elation *and* melancholy. When we are in the midst of our grief, exposure to the type of art that inspires us can smooth out the rough edges of the pain. "It's not that pain equals art. It's that creativity has the power to look pain in the eye, and decide to turn it into something better," wrote Susan Cain, in her brilliant book *Bittersweet*.[7] This kind of "inspiration exposure" will aid readers in transcending grief through the often-unseen beauty of our deepest emotions. Art encourages healing through inventiveness and imagination.

The arts also provide the glue that bonds us all together in a shared community of sufferable brotherhood. When we see ourselves on-screen, hear a lyric that was written just for us, learn that the ancients asked the same questions, or experience any number of examples from history and art—we feel seen and understood. We know that we are not alone. Our pain and experience are mirrored back to us, and it is somehow shared with others. Art is a constant, consummate lifelong friend. Even in our darkest moments, art creates glimmers of light that give us hope.

> EVEN IN OUR DARKEST MOMENTS, ART CREATES GLIMMERS OF LIGHT THAT GIVE US HOPE.

The majestic grandeur and healing power

INTRODUCTION

of nature is also important in our rewriting journey. Like art, it has the ability to inspire, draw us out of ourselves, and connect us to something bigger. I will use examples from both the arts and nature to show how they have helped my grief experience and to encourage you to use them in yours.

No matter who you are, you have likely been touched by experiences in life that are deeply unpleasant. As a result, you've stored the mournful memories of these experiences in the recesses of your mind and heart. The inner pain is always there. Art, nature, and music give you permission to feel that inner pain without any shame. They allow you to be human for a few moments.

A NEW WAY OF THINKING ABOUT GRIEF

It may be difficult to consider while going through it, but grief can be an opportunity. Grief means we cared for and loved others. It means we were touched by experiences from the past that defined who we are today. Grief means we accepted and lived through the often-frightening inescapability of change. These deep feelings are not to be discarded or forgotten. Embracing our sadness is an opportunity not only to live in the present but to be lifted up beyond our own imagination. Loss is a natural and certain part of life, yet many of us don't have the tools to cope with it. If we can learn to live with as much faith in the sorrowful as in the happy aspects of living, our lives will be vastly different.

INTRODUCTION

In this book, I'm going to equip you for moving through the grief experience by helping you find the magic in your tragic. We're going to flip the script on traditional bereavement and find new ways forward.

In chapter 1, we'll look for the dignity in suffering and see how there is beauty to be found in even the darkest places. In chapter 2, we'll move from sadness to inspiration by reauthoring the tragedies of life as exquisite experiential benefits we are lucky to have felt. In chapters 3 and 4, we'll see the power of connecting with something outside ourselves, and we will explore the strength of healthy aloneness. Chapters 5 and 6 examine depression and anxiety, which often go hand in hand with grief. In chapter 7 we'll examine the concept of "closure" and why we are so reluctant to address grief. Chapters 8 and 9 offer practical coping techniques like mindfulness and self-regulation skills. In chapter 10, the often-overlooked concepts of healthy "nostalgia" and "daydreaming" are examined. And in chapters 11 and 12, we'll look at how to maintain resilience through human vulnerability and learning to go with the flow of life.

To survive the rigors of the modern world and perhaps to procure a degree of happiness, we must be flexible and turn toward our suffering while avoiding the temptation to turn away from what is painful. That type of flexibility can transform our discomfort into other qualities like openness, curiosity, and

> WE'LL LOOK FOR THE DIGNITY IN SUFFERING AND SEE HOW THERE IS BEAUTY TO BE FOUND IN EVEN THE DARKEST PLACES.

self-compassion. It can increase the possibility of feeling lighter and more fulfilled in our life.

I hope that by reading this book, you can find inspiration amid grief and develop a similar appreciation for the *magic in the tragic*.

CHAPTER 1

DISCOVERING THE DIGNITY IN SUFFERING

Seeing the Beauty Within the Beast

The wound is the place where the light enters you.
RUMI

IF WE'RE GOING TO BUILD OUR EMOTIONAL RESILIENCE, WE will need to get profoundly acquainted with the practice of discovering the beauty in suffering. Many of us are quick to frame suffering as bad, to think of loss as the enemy, and for good reason. It's disheartening. It hurts. But when we give suffering dignity, when we associate it with beauty instead of shame, fear, or desperation, we can change the narrative of our pain. We can find beauty in the beast.

THE MAGIC IN THE TRAGIC

Pain and suffering are as natural to being human as laughter and joy. So is our aversion to pain. We don't want to suffer! Spiritual teacher Eckhart Tolle said it best: "Nothing could be more normal than an unwillingness to suffer. Yet if you can let go of that unwillingness and instead allow the pain to be there, you may notice a subtle inner separation from the pain."[1] Basically, if we can get more comfortable with seeing pain as normal and natural, if we can trust our wounds as conduits of light, we will be able to mitigate the pain in the long run.

> FINDING THE MAGIC IN THE TRAGIC IS ABOUT DISCOVERING THE DIGNITY IN SUFFERING AND HONORING GRIEF.

Finding the *magic in the tragic* is about discovering the dignity in suffering and honoring grief. When it comes to human pain—which everyone avoids but knows they will someday endure—discovering the dignity in suffering helps transform it into something different. Grief then becomes associated with splendor and wonderment instead of fear and avoidance. These are prerequisites for adapting to our changing world and getting through hard times ahead. No matter how badly we are emotionally triggered by difficult events and emotions, we can develop the skills to calm our worries and breathe through the pain.

DIGNITY IN SUFFERING ON THE STAGE

The ancient Greeks gave us a valuable example. They were no strangers to loss and calamity, enduring perpetual war and strife. And yet they learned how to transcend grief and process the pains of life through what David Brooks called a "tragic sensibility." This was a sensibility that "taught resilience and anti-fragility—to be prepared for the pain that will inevitably come."[2]

We see how the Greeks responded to suffering via the instructive art of drama. *Tragedy,* from the Greek *tragodia,* (which originally meant "goat-song"[3]), a dramatic poem or play in formal language, is the mode of many classical Greek dramas from playwrights like Sophocles, Euripides, and Aeschylus. The ancient plays, derived from the concept of a "tragic song," were traditionally intended to summon a *catharsis*, a process of pain that awakens rapture. Essentially, they dealt with sorrow by playing it out on stage. Via their own method of grief therapy, they helped audiences heal and learn lessons about the nobility of suffering—a nobility that came from the pride one felt for *having* suffered. They deliberately respected and elevated human pain instead of circumventing it.

According to Aristotle, Greek tragedies were "an invitation of the suffering intended in effecting the proper purgation or catharsis of emotions."[4] They used drama and the arts to cleanse away the ills of life. The ancient Greeks were responsible for many philosophical, scientific, political, and artistic achievements that shape our world today, but the way they transmuted psychic pain to soothe human sorrow and help awaken rapture is perhaps their greatest contribution.

A millennium and a half later, William Shakespeare's young Danish prince, Hamlet, would poetically refer to the pains of life as "the thousand natural shocks that flesh is heir to."[5] In Hamlet we see a medieval understanding of tragedy, nobility in death, and catharsis. In the iconic play, Hamlet valorizes his grief over his father's murder by pondering deep questions about his suffering. In the end, his introspection—sparked by his confusion and sorrow—assists him in solving his problems and bringing stability back to Denmark's ruling family. The brooding prince takes action against adversity by paying tribute to his pain, not by escaping it.

OUR PERCEPTION OF THINGS

If grief increases the sensitivity of the heart, as it did for the ancient Greeks, it can also instruct the heart, teaching it valuable lessons. In *The Prophet*, one of the bestselling books of all time, Kahlil Gibran teaches us about grief: "Your pain is the breaking of the shell that encloses your understanding."[6] Breaking open the "shell of understanding" is one of the foundations of building resilience. One way to start that process is to notice everyday things we hear and see with different ears and eyes, which we will explore more later in the chapter. The lessons are already within us, but a new perception of them can help us identify them better.

For instance, pay close attention the next time you have an emotional reaction to a favorite song, a meaningful passage in a book, a famous quotation, an exquisite painting, or even an experience in nature. Ask yourself: *Why am I so affected? Why* did the hair on the back of my neck stand up? Why does my elation feel like a confirmation of my unexpressed emotions of sorrow, sadness, and even fear? And in the moment, why does it also feel like someone or something knows exactly what I am feeling? The alchemy of the senses has more power than we know.

Perhaps we are so deeply touched because sadness doesn't necessarily make us depressed—but happiness can. This is called the *happiness paradox*, which is the notion that always pursuing happiness can actually make you feel *less* happy. Anytime we rigorously pursue happiness, we infer that we don't have it. So we deprive ourselves of the happiness that exists right now.

Happiness is fleeting. Sometimes we feel sad because, unconsciously, we sense that the feeling of joy won't last. Could it be that human pain is inextricably linked to the experience of feeling happy followed by the disappointing recognition of that happy feeling ending? If so, there is joy in the knowledge that in any unhappy moment, the feeling of pain will end as well. They are two sides of the same coin. They cannot exist without each other. Acknowledging and accepting this paradox is the beginning of understanding the pain *and* the rapture. This is seeing the beauty within the beast.

> THE ALCHEMY OF THE SENSES HAS MORE POWER THAN WE KNOW.

For me, hearing the comforting sound of Wolfgang Amadeus Mozart's piano concerto *Elvira Madigan* has always felt like the voice of the Almighty reassuring me that I am not alone.[7] It's as if the universe is telling me, *Everything is going to be okay.*

We all react differently to the idea of inviting in pain, in the hope of admitting beauty alongside it. Some people say that after a loss, the ensuing human suffering is one of the few times we allow ourselves to be vulnerable. It gives us consent to express our pain openly and even let our tears gush. But for others, expressing grief with family and friends can be tricky, and so can entering willingly into places of vulnerability. People close to us hate to see us suffer, and they might shift into "fixer" mode or instruct us to "get over it." After some time, they root us on: *Learn to forget! It's time to move on!*

The problem is it's almost impossible to do that. We don't just decide to move on and it just happens. And it's not the healthiest thing to try either. Our well-intentioned people can't always see that we need to endure some of the pain if we are to find a path to joy. In the end, it's not about fighting, forgetting, or moving on. It's more about honoring the feelings of sadness and holding them in high regard. It's about viewing grief as an opportunity to learn, to evolve, and to be more resilient. "The deeper the sorrow carves into your being, the more joy you can contain," said Gibran.[8]

PAYING HOMAGE TO SORROW WITH MUSIC AND ART

If we can't always be vulnerable with others—because we don't feel safe or understood, or because our culture doesn't permit society to be completely honest about how we feel, especially

DISCOVERING THE DIGNITY IN SUFFERING

around sadness—we can certainly learn to internally pay homage to our melancholy feelings. Through the awareness of the beauty all around us, we rely on the often unspoken grandeur that could not exist without its tragic complement. Let me give you an example.

The late-nineteenth-century French composer Claude Debussy wrote superbly delicate and sorrowful music that has magic in its gentle qualities. His composition style was at first criticized for its formlessness and labeled too "impressionistic"[9]—a reckless leap from the conventional thematic musical structures of the time. However, today his discrete tonal ambiguities and ethereal, free-floating melodies are respectably distinguished and easily recognizable.

In 1890 Debussy was inspired by the poems of writer Paul Verlaine in his collection titled *Fêtes Galantes*. Debussy was particularly taken by a short poem in the collection called "Clair de Lune," or "Moonlight" in English.[10] It led to Debussy composing one of the most memorable pieces of classic music ever produced, also called "Clair de Lune."[11]

Paul Verlaine's poetic words inspired Debussy's music:

> The still moonlight, sad and beautiful,
> That sets the birds dreaming in the trees
> And the fountains sobbing in ecstasy.[12]

Although Verlaine's words are simple, Debussy's musical interpretation of this stanza is breathtaking. The sincere poignancy of "Clair de Lune" possesses such a marked quality of pathos and sensibility that it's hard not to have your emotions aroused. When I listen to it, I don't just hear it, I experience it. Time stands still. The piece alters my brain chemistry like a high dose of antidepressant medication. It links me to the cosmic connection of universal belonging that elevates my soul. And then, suddenly, everything I grieved about two minutes ago is replaced with reflective gratitude.

The somber, atmospheric beauty in "Clair de Lune" helps me understand some of the obscurities of my complicated heart, the difficult times I endured in my life, and all the people I have loved and lost. Goodwill toward all human beings floods my spirit. The effect is analogous to the experience that Susan Cain reported after she heard a piece of affecting music: "What I feel, really, is love: a great tidal outpouring of it. A deep kinship with all the other souls in the world who know the sorrow that music strains to express."[13]

Another instance of paying homage to sadness I find embedded in the paintings of Vincent van Gogh. We would be hard-pressed to find another historical figure more associated with human suffering. His life and artwork are salient examples from someone who changed his response to the world around him, despite terrible hardship and appalling life conditions. The chronic mental illness, loneliness, social alienation, poverty, and many other misfortunes he endured are staggering, and yet through his distinctive, evocative art he transcended tragedy.

The lives of tormented artists have always intrigued us, as we've seen in such Hollywood films as *Pollock*, starring Ed

DISCOVERING THE DIGNITY IN SUFFERING

Harris, *Amadeus* with Tom Hulce, and *Frida* played by Salma Hayek. But no artist has garnered more entranced attention than Van Gogh. Kirk Douglas, in the 1956 film *Lust for Life*, established the predominant image of the post-impressionist artist: a tortured virtuoso, helpless in the grip of artistic brilliance that no one could appreciate. Van Gogh was simply born too early to be valued. Society in nineteenth-century Europe had little to offer him in terms of mental health treatment, medication, support, therapy, or even a viable market for selling his paintings.

Nevertheless, why does Van Gogh's art move us so much? His paintings still have the same striking, aesthetic impact on the eyes of millions of people today, perhaps because he *did* suffer so much adversity in his young life. Does this make the tragic more emphatic?

When I look at certain Van Gogh paintings, I synchronously feel an indirect current of buoyancy surge through my body, not because of the prominent hues and stunning scenes of the French countryside, but because of the often complex, touching sadness they represent. The contrasting evocative images of utter beauty against the backdrop of his misery is astonishing.

Many of us also resonate with Van Gogh's feelings of rejection. In fact, the more absorbing and lively his paintings are, the more we feel his pain. Here's where the optimism lies: Because he suffered so profoundly with mental illness and because he lived in a world that did not accept him, Van Gogh was compelled to create a fantasy world that was kinder to him—a world that didn't forsake him. In order to survive, perhaps he chose to imagine a world where he was free of his mental illness; his dreamlike paintings were how he decided he *would* experience the world—enchanting, aesthetic, benevolent. In other words, Van Gogh's eccentric, dreamlike depictions of life represent the kind of reality that he wished he existed in.[14] Was art his escape? Or was it a necessary coping technique? Or both?

The art he created was his only way of communicating how much he hurt inside. As a result, the transcendence I feel in the presence of his art encourages me to appreciate how far I have come amid my own hard times. Plainly said, his well-fought struggles assist me in being gentler to myself. His grief allows me to give myself compassion for my own suffering and—when the opportunity is right—communicate that pain to others.

> ART AND MUSIC CAN REMIND US THAT WE ARE NOT ALONE IN OUR SUFFERING.

Whether we listen to "Clair de Lune," look at a Van Gogh painting, or find another source of inspiration, art and music can remind us that we are not alone in our suffering, and it can give us a place to feel our feelings deeply.

COMPASSION AND VULNERABILITY IN SUFFERING

One of the hardest things in allowing ourselves to feel our suffering deeply is to show ourselves compassion in the process. In his book *Resilient*, Rick Hanson, PhD, defined compassion as the "recognition of pain with the desire to relieve it—which can be given to oneself as much as it can to others."[15] Van Gogh's paintings have a permission-giving quality—he put his anguish on display. Van Gogh bore his lifelong suffering as best he could, despite the unimaginable circumstances he was born into, by painting his pain and relieving it through art.

Wheatfield with Crows, one of his last paintings, has an ominous quality to it. Large crows, perhaps prophetically, fly over a golden wheatfield in Auvers-sur-Oise, France, where he painted many of his most memorable works. The painting is yet another fine example of bridging the gap between his troubled mental state and the pastoral beauty that surrounded him. In a letter to his brother Theo in July 1890, he referred briefly to his isolation amid the scenic landscapes that gave him so much inspiration: "There are vast fields of wheat under turbulent skies, and I did not need to go out of my way to try to express sadness and extreme loneliness."[16]

With a mind that betrayed him so often, Van Gogh must have gone through hell trying to establish a semblance of sanity. It's remarkable to imagine that on his most incapacitated days he could even take the time to go out to the fields, mix paint on his palette, hold a paintbrush in his hand, and push through the chaos swirling in his head. *That* moves me. That moves me for anyone else who feels even a modicum of mental disturbance. We can all use Van Gogh's

> WE MUST TRY TO LOOK FOR THE SPLENDOR IN THE GRIEF AND THE HOPEFULNESS IN THE ADVERSITY.

story as a way to build resilience the next time we feel overwhelmed with our upsets and losses. Just as he did, we must try to look for the splendor in the grief and the hopefulness in the adversity.

THE POWER OF NATURE

Another way of tapping into the collective frequency of joy within human suffering is by looking up at the stars at night. When I see that I am an infinitesimal fleck on a diminutive planet hurtling through space, at first it makes me feel lonely and insignificant. I am disappointed by the profound isolation, and I am trapped in my own echo chamber of earthly worries and petty responsibilities. What if my sorrow, suffering, loneliness, and grief are all part of an enormous life-cycle mechanism that is unknowable to me? It's enough to make my head spin.

But then I become aware of this overwhelming understanding: Despite the fact that I feel so small, and that I am overshadowed by the eerie limitlessness of the universe containing billions of other planets and stars, I am part of something vastly superior to me. And because I can't explain or comprehend it, this notion gives me comfort.

Writer R. J. Anderson expounded: "Even though I was a tiny speck in an infinite cosmos, a blip on the timeline of eternity, I was not without purpose."[17] In the spaces between recognizing my minuteness as mere space-dust and acknowledging the curious wonder of what our existence is all about, I turn to my trusted sources of inspiration. I stay enlightened as best I can. Claude Debussy, Vincent van Gogh, and the ancient Greeks are partly responsible for that.

> I TURN TO MY TRUSTED SOURCES OF INSPIRATION. I STAY ENLIGHTENED AS BEST I CAN.

TRY THIS PRACTICE

Inspiration Exposure

In a simple exercise that helps us practice "inspiration exposure," we can take a quick inventory of what moves us. It's quite easy.

Write down the following:

- A favorite song (any genre)
- A favorite piece of art (painting, sculpture, anything creative)
- A favorite quote
- A favorite movie
- A favorite place in nature (for example, a lake you spent summers swimming in, a beach you vacationed at, a special camping spot in the woods, a favorite hiking trail)

For each answer, ask yourself the following. Be as specific as possible.

- Why do the tones or lyrics of this song touch me so deeply?
- Why does this piece of art inspire me so much?
- What is so meaningful about this quote I chose?
- What themes (or memories) in this movie stir my heart so deeply?
- What is the feeling this favorite place in nature evokes in me?

Remember, it's easy to undervalue the evocative feelings these favorite things induce in us. In the words of astrophysicist and author Neil deGrasse Tyson, "The world needs poets. Not to interpret what is plain and obvious, but to help us take pause and reflect on the beauty of people, places, and ideas—things we might otherwise take for granted."[18]

If your answers above give you joy, if they excite you and give you chills, and especially if they cause a little sadness or nostalgia, you might be plugged into that often unheard frequency I've been talking about. The "something" that gets awakened in you, that alchemy of the senses, that *magic in the tragic* is perhaps affecting you positively. And the more you embrace it, the more you glorify it, the more you will see it manifest in other areas of your life. But most significantly, you will learn to see the beauty within the beast of your own suffering.

Keep your "inspiration" answers handy, either written down on paper or saved on your smart phone or computer. Amid your daily dramas and conflicts, your passing griefs and uproars, take a few minutes to check in with them, reconnect with them, and allow them to move you. This practice will help remind you that whatever struggles you're grappling with in the moment, there are beautiful *and* sorrowful things that can equally give you strength. Over time, the exercise will align you with the indispensable benefit of appreciating the dignity in suffering.

CHAPTER 2

REAUTHORING OUR WOUNDS

Moving from Sadness to Inspiration

We generally change ourselves for one of two reasons: inspiration or desperation.

JIM ROHN, PARAPHRASED

IN MY PRIVATE PRACTICE, MANY PATIENTS COME TO SEE ME after suffering a devastating loss. For some, the context of their wounds becomes part of a storyline, an unquestioned inner dialogue they adopt as truth. Sometimes the inner dialogue is enveloped in a shroud of hopelessness that leaves them feeling desperate: *I'll never be happy again. I can't survive without him/her. I have nothing to live for.*

As we think about flipping the script on grief, I suggest we recognize constructive aching and positive wounding as ways to move us from sadness to inspiration. What does it mean to experience *constructive aching*? Or to endure *positive wounding*? At first glance, these both sound like frivolous oxymorons, like jumbo shrimp, an intimate stranger, or a civil war. In reality, however, these terms are helpful frameworks for approaching and reauthoring grief.

Constructive aching is our ability to use the unavoidable ills of grief in a way that benefits us and contributes to personal growth. Positive wounding is acknowledging that our past and perhaps future wounds have a healthy purpose, instead of seeing them one-dimensionally as things we should have avoided.

Our wounds and heartbreak may hurt us, but they can also help us. Pain humbles us, and only by experiencing it can we begin to understand that grief is one of humankind's most profound and important rites of passage. "As human beings, we are both essentially whole and relatively wounded," said author John J. Prendergast, PhD, in his book *The Deep Heart: Our Portal to Presence*.[1] He explained how accessing and trusting the depths of our inner self is like doing a deep dive. The plunge helps us establish and build emotional resilience by better acquainting ourselves with the often unseen landscape and texture of our psyche. This can help us come to terms with, and even benefit from, devastating loss. It can balance the pain of tragedy with the knowledge that we are learning and evolving from it.

How does a person feel deeply wounded yet whole at the

same time? As a starting place, they'll need to be open to feeling pain and discomfort and to move through it by taking risks and being vulnerable. No one likes that option, and rightly so. Opening yourself up to vulnerability is itself an act of faith and courage. But getting comfortable with discomfort is a good place to start.

> OPENING YOURSELF UP TO VULNERABILITY IS ITSELF AN ACT OF FAITH AND COURAGE.

The loss, the wound, the scar are all marks of grief, and examining them is necessary if we are to build resilience and experience ultimate relief. If we lean into, instead of run away from, our pain, we can rewire ourselves to be moved by sadness. This alteration of the common narrative—the one that tells us sadness is nothing but misery from which no benefit can be derived—leads us to pliability and possibility. It helps us see our pain not just as unnecessary suffering but as *constructive aching* and *positive wounding*. We can rewrite a tragic situation not as a miserable end but as a promising beginning. So learning to be moved and inspired by sadness means acquiring the skill to give yourself chills as often as possible. We all have the ability to do that.

REWRITING MY OWN GRIEF

As a boy, I had an insecure attachment to my parents, an anxious type of human-relating characterized by a number of traits such as worry, clinginess, and an inability to trust.

Despite loving them dearly, I was unable to form a solid, reliable base of safety in their presence. Perhaps the cause was environmental or a genetic inclination. Or both. At any rate, this affected my ability to be closely connected to them and others too.

When I learned that death inevitably comes to everyone someday, my innocent, preadolescent mind could not handle it. I could not bear the thought of my parents dying, ever. As the Hebrew philosopher and poet Yehuda Halevi wrote, "'Tis a fearful thing to love what death can touch."[2]

My bond with them, in spite of its own complications and disappointments, meant everything to me. I suffered seemingly endless dark nights alone in bed, fearful of the day they would be taken from me. I was too afraid to divulge my trepidation to anyone, least of all to my parents. According to child psychologist Alice Miller, I experienced "forbidden suffering—a potentially devastating phenomenon that traumatizes children who feel they are not permitted to express their pain."[3] Although I could not articulate my feelings at the time, I cursed the heavens for burdening me with the human inclination to love so intensely. It seemed to me my life was rigged, and it all seemed so unfair. I felt utterly alone in my torment.

In October 2004, the day finally came—two days, to be precise—in which my worst fears were realized. Both my parents, who had long since divorced and lived a thousand miles apart, fell ill and entered hospice care. They died thirteen days apart. Both had been sick, my mother from cancer and my father, twenty years her senior, from age-related complications. At sixty-four, my beautiful mother, who had always been joyful and full of life, passed away. My father died as he had lived, proud and detached. I was consumed by the indescribable grief I had feared from a young age. The cruelty of life all but suffocated me, just as I had known it would. I unconsciously decided I would not, could not, ever recover from such inevitable catastrophe. For years after my parents' deaths, I wallowed in my grief. My worst fears had come true. I was alone with my sadness. What could be worse?

But then, miraculously, my once-dreaded fear became a soul-maturing journey that gave way to a new realization about death. My worst fear ultimately evolved into one of the greatest gifts of my life. Unwanted grief gave way to unexpressed love. I had loved my parents so deeply but had not been able to express it, until grief gave me the opportunity. Without grief's informative nature, I might never have understood love at all.

Today, Halevi's poem no longer haunts me. Instead, I draw relief from it. "To love what death can touch" is not something to dread but something to embrace. It's a heartfelt, genuine approach to life that honors the value of loving and losing.

Even though there was pain in my loss, and even more pain in the lost opportunities of not being able to express my love while my parents were alive, I take comfort in the constructive aching. One of the last lines of Halevi's poem helps me to appreciate the loving bond I *did* have with my parents instead of just remembering the unpleasant nature of their passing and the fact that I'd never see them again. "To remember this brings painful joy."[4]

The "painful joy" of remembering deceased loved ones I believed I could not live without has been most instructive. The fire I passed through and the heartache that I endured elevated my understanding of grief to new heights that I never imagined possible. Today I treasure my wounds and I feel, on some level, proud of my transcendence of them. Constructive aching has brought my life more meaning. For one thing, it soothed my fear of the unknown regarding death because I passed through it. But more importantly, I now see my parents' deaths as an initiation to becoming a better, more adaptable person. But the only way that happened was through my conscious decision to feel the pain. The constructive aching lies in the application of the aesthetic to the grief—the auspicious pairing of their deaths with the beauty of the lesson.

OUR SADNESS PROMPTS EMPATHY

Grasping and embracing the sadness of loss brings us closer to others who have experienced similar pain. The average person cannot begin to comprehend another's pain unless they experience it themselves. We don't *know* until we know. Most of us feel some sympathy for someone who is in physical or emotional pain, but until we live through a similar experience, until we have empathy, the feeling remains vague and intangible, placing us merely on the fringe of "getting" the authenticity of that person's pain. We are not there yet. Positive wounds connect us to each other and are valuable and necessary.

Call it spiritual or a natural phenomenon of being human, but the shift from sympathy to empathy is crucial to acknowledging something outside ourselves. We realize we are not in control and we are part of something much bigger. That shouldn't make us feel powerless, but rather, over time, it can help to empower us because we can let go of what we can't change or control. Even more importantly, it unites us in a cosmic connection to others who have experienced the same thing.

Consider if you woke up every morning with a degree of expectation that there would be some form of discomfort, stress, or even grief throughout the day. As strange as it may sound, it would actually make the day go easier. But we don't like that principle. We want the seductive assurance that the day will go as planned, what Buddhists refer to as our attachment to the illusion of permanence.[5] That desire for life to play out perfectly, with no hiccups or bumps along the way, is why we suffer. We all endure the ache of disappointment and impermanence every day. No one is spared and that's a good thing. It connects us to each other and opens us up to empathy.

Pema Chödrön spoke of how awareness of suffering is something we all share and what unites us all. In her book *How We Live Is How We Die*, she explained it profoundly: "No one is indifferent to their own suffering. . . . In this essential way, everyone—now and through the course of time—is exactly like ourselves. We all want to be free from any form of pain."[6]

> EXPERIENCING EMOTIONAL PAIN EXPANDS OUR ABILITY TO UNDERSTAND OTHERS AND BE MORE COMPASSIONATE.

And because we all share this universal experience, grief draws us closer to others and teaches us empathy. Experiencing emotional pain expands our ability to understand others and be more compassionate. It helps us open our hearts to others. Without firsthand experience, we have only a theoretical concept of someone else's pain.

If we first acquire the emotional suppleness to hold our own difficult feelings and thoughts, facing them with care and then using them to kindle positive change, it opens up the likelihood of honestly commiserating with another.

When we are in the presence of another person's suffering similar to ours and when we connect over that commonality, we not only feel validated, but we feel hopeful again.

A few decades ago, as a group therapy facilitator at a psychiatric hospital in Los Angeles, I witnessed up close the power of shared empathy. The raw and honest interpersonal relating between group participants helped to significantly reduce their anxiety and elevate their moods. The fellowship they created was often more efficacious than the therapeutic interventions and educational information I offered them. After just a few sessions, many of the groups coalesced into a viable ecosystem of support. And it was not uncommon for group participants to continue supporting one another even after their treatment terms ended.

If we feel empathy for others and can put ourselves in their shoes, we will be better prepared for when tragedy strikes us. And, by virtue of association, it gives us permission to be vulnerable as well (we will discuss the importance of vulnerability in a later chapter). This process of learning from others and ourselves through experience keeps humanity joined together. When we commit to observing and experiencing our feelings of grief as often as we can, we improve our accessibility to that fellowship. Grief offers us solidarity and the prospect for unanimity with others on a community and even global level. It links and binds us across race, political affiliation, and social and economic status.

FROM SADNESS TO INSPIRATION

The American artist Andrew Wyeth was a master of observing the suppleness of emotion. By tapping into the cohesive element of emotional struggle that joins all humanity, he was inspired by the touching life and uncommon spirit of a woman named Christina Olson. His iconic 1948 painting, *Christina's World*, is the best known of several pieces that featured a mysterious woman who lived in a nearby farmhouse in Cushing, Maine. It's documented that the middle-aged Christina suffered from a degenerative muscular disease that rendered her unable to walk and largely immobile. Disability, however, did not compromise Ms. Olson's will and determination to experience life and to thrive. Rather than use a wheelchair, she often opted to crawl where she wanted to go.[7]

THE MAGIC IN THE TRAGIC

Christina's World exudes an unmistakably soft and rustic serenity with a quiet, moving sadness on its own. The idyllic yet desolate rural landscape, with its earthy tones and unimposing sky, quickly draws viewers' attention to a lone human figure: a woman in a pink dress lying in a grassy field facing away from the viewer and toward a farmhouse on a hill. The faceless, solitary woman captivates the imagination. Who is she? What is she doing there? Looking more closely, a careful observer will see the woman's body is uneasily curved, and her arms and hands appear tense as if struggling to support her upper torso. The woman seems fiercely attentive, either to the view of the house or to some other enigmatic purpose. The viewer is unsure if she is helplessly beckoning for assistance or attempting to independently crawl to her destination. Both options seem cruel and perhaps heartless, but nonetheless, intriguing. There is a sublime and almost narcotic beauty to her imagined suffering, and yet, it is inspiring. Why?

According to Wyeth, the painting depicts Christina's inner world symbolically as a literal uphill battle.[8] She is solitary in her paralytic journey, perhaps straining to achieve her goal of reaching the farmhouse, which sits perched on the hill like a lighthouse in the dark of her night. The "world" Wyeth portrays might be a place of the emotional depth of not only Christina's internal world but a world many of us have experienced too. The painting is a figurative representation of the arduous trials and challenges of being human. For countless numbers of people in the world, Ms. Olson's world of struggle and strife on a day-to-day basis is not so rare. Just making it to the next day, every day is remarkable. There is courage and integrity in regularly choosing to accept one's predicament so gracefully.

Christina's World moves us from sadness to inspiration and successfully captures the magic in the tragic. The grief of her condition, the difficulty of living life with a chronic disability, is indisputably portrayed, yet the poetry of the image is stirring. Wyeth helps us feel her pain.

EMOTIONAL PAIN GETS US USED TO DISCOMFORT

Permitting ourselves to feel emotional pain also makes us more effective in our daily activities. It makes us stronger by raising our distress tolerance thresholds and allowing us to get used to the discomfort more easily. "It is easy to imagine that attempts to eliminate pain and weakness in daily life could lead to a sort of emotional allergy, that when hard times come and someone feels grief or fear that is impossible to ignore, the person will not have the tools to face these feelings," wrote Arthur C. Books in his book *From Strength to Strength*.[9] If we familiarize ourselves with sadness and pain on some level, we give ourselves tools when it comes stronger, harder, unexpected.

It's like the cold swimming pool analogy or the polar, icy plunge in the dead of winter: If you jump into any body of cold water (or a cold shower), and you splash around in the water long enough, after a while, the water starts to feel warmer even though the temperature has not changed. Your brain acclimates to the cold and, on some level, normalizes it. The same is true for the heart when it comes to adaptability and the cold waters of grief. Most people can adjust to anything if they sit in it long enough.

This may sound like an exercise in brutality, but learning to raise our tolerance to pain helps us move toward an understanding of, and appreciation for, the beauty in it. If growing and evolving is the payoff, then the ephemeral moments of utter distress begin to feel valuable. Like Christina in Wyeth's painting, we gain strength through our own weakness. Consider, for a moment, the mind shift at play here: *Gaining strength through weakness.* Such a revelation upends the narrative that emotional vulnerability is weakness and leaves room for the potential to teach our reflexes to bypass our aversion to distress by replacing it with *curiosity* about our distress.

> WE GAIN STRENGTH THROUGH OUR OWN WEAKNESS.

In her book *Unbinding the Soul*, B. Raven Lee considered recognizing the power of pain to build resilience. She said that awareness of our pain is "allowing us to view our tragedies and losses not simply as ends but as new beginnings, junctures for the potential for personal growth."[10] To me, life can be seen as a cycle of perpetuity—a series of beginnings *and* endings. If we are going to learn how to tolerate the endings, it helps to know there is always a beginning just around the corner. Naturally this alleviates the sting of a painful ending but also establishes the empowering understanding that life's ups and downs are on a continuum. They are not fixed.

REAUTHORING OUR GRIEF

While awful events can occur in our lives, they don't necessarily have to leave us emotionally fragmented. The wounds we carry remind us of how deeply we are affected and, more importantly, how we understand our suffering.

A great image of this is in the Japanese art of kintsugi, which mends shattered pottery in a beautiful way. After the broken pieces are put back together with lacquer, they are then painted over with gold and silver. *Kintsugi* means "to join with gold,"[11] and the art form highlights the cracks and broken pieces instead of minimizing them. The broken lines are in fact what make the pottery distinctly beautiful and original, rebirthed as a new creation from an imperfect past.

What a powerful analogy for our lives. Like kintsugi, we can put ourselves back together with our cracks on display by modifying the narrative of the tragic events we experience. We can change our future by reauthoring our past. We can build strength and resilience by recognizing and respecting the imperfect.

Think of a physical scar on your body that is now permanently visible on the surface of your skin. Whether it's a recent wound or a time-worn one from childhood, the scar is a symbol of how "badly" you were once injured. Or is it? Maybe you see your scar as a symbol of how much you've healed and recovered despite the experience and the indelible mark left by it. An emotional wound is similar, though it might be harder to grasp its essence because we can't physically see it. But these are the wounds and scars well worth our attention, and creating a new narrative around them may require effort and patience.

> WHATEVER STORIES YOU HAVE BEEN TELLING YOURSELF ABOUT THE EXPERIENCE AND THE MARK(S) LEFT BY IT ARE JUST THAT—STORIES.

Take a moment to consider any one of your emotional scars. Now realize that whatever stories you have been telling yourself about the experience and the mark(s) left by it are just that—stories. They may be abstract, unverifiable tales and voices appearing and often masquerading as facts. As mentioned earlier in the chapter, our narratives of our past wounds and scars can be like errant conspiracy theories. We conjure them up, we "write them," we animatedly tell them to ourselves and others, sometimes over and over, and they become more cemented with each telling. Though it may be difficult to admit, we might even feel proud of them. We might occasionally take them down from their shelves and polish them like precious artifacts—souvenirs and badges that represent our battles and inform the world of the misfortune we have endured, and ultimately represent our tremendous fortitude. These, we often believe, are stories well worthy of pity from ourselves and others. The unfortunate truth of these stories is that they can be

REAUTHORING OUR WOUNDS

self-radicalized, and we might only believe them because it has never occurred to us to challenge them. We may have resorted to accepting them as fate. But nothing is a foregone conclusion. Our stories can be retold, and doing so creates tremendous potential for growth and change.

My first therapist, psychologist Dr. Claire Ciliotta, used to tell me that I had no business judging myself based on my past. She taught me that if I want to move forward in my life, I must remember that the only person I am destined to become is the person I choose to be today, right now. The rest of my history prior to today was an assumption, which led me to misleading negative conclusions about myself that had no foundation and no place in my future. In other words, why look back? You're not going in that direction anyway.

What if you could learn to transcribe a new narrative? It could be a redemption narrative or even a forgiveness one. Or you may learn to reauthor the story you have been telling yourself *about* yourself. Perhaps finding new meaning regarding your past. Finding the good in you that will sustain you better than the old yarns you've been believing for years. But to emerge from the ashes of your past, you first must acknowledge, as with the philosophy of kintsugi, the radiance in the grief and the delicate, broken pieces of yourself.

TRY THIS PRACTICE

Change Your Narrative

Think of one or two adverse events in your recent past that were emotionally difficult and caused you to cling to a story about them. For instance, they could be situations that you feel terribly guilty about; situations where you were personally wounded, like from an intimate relationship or a family conflict; or a time of loss and tragedy that you had no control over. This exercise will help you begin the process of changing that narrative to a more compassionate and resilient one.

After you have chosen your events or situations, start thinking about the current narrative you have attached to each story. Chances are, your narrative has not been serving you well and has created a false, negative predisposition.

Step 1: Describe the narrative of the event. Make sure it's not more than one or two sentences. Be as specific as possible.

Step 2: Ask yourself: How is this story serving me? Is it helping me be more resilient? Or making me feel worse about it?

Step 3: Ask yourself: Is the story based on concrete facts? Or is the story based on my opinion or interpretation of the event?

Step 4: Write the new narrative and replace the old one in one or two sentences.

To help you come up with your alternative narrative, remember to see adversity as a heartening agent, to discover optimism in suffering. Keep in mind the propositions of allowing *positive wounding* and learning from *constructive aching*.

Another thing that might help is to pretend you are helping a family member or close friend reauthor a negative story they have been clinging to. As you consider your narrative, pretend it pains you to watch this person suffer with their old story (which you know may not even be true). What would you say to them? How would you help them reframe the situation without the bias they are holding on to?

Here is an example of an interpretive story about a recent painful breakup with an intimate other:

I've never felt this much pain before. Something must be wrong with me. Why do I have to suffer so much? The pain is unbearable. I am a failure in love.

And here is an example of reauthoring the same painful breakup as a heartening agent that seeks the optimism in the suffering:

Today, I choose to see the splendor in my pain. I choose to focus on the beauty of my sorrow because in the long run, it will enhance compassion for myself and others. The more I allow myself to feel emotional pain, the more I can rely on myself to get through it in the future.

Here is another example of a negative personal narrative about your career that is not serving you well:

I just got passed up for a promotion at work. That confirms what I have always believed: I will never succeed. Others will move up in the company because they are smarter than me and more deserving. Why bother trying anymore? It's hopeless.

And here is a reauthoring of the same career disappointment as an example of constructive aching that helps to build optimism in suffering:

Wait, stop, I am jumping to conclusions. Getting passed up at work hurts, but it's not the complete picture of me. My career doesn't define me. Perhaps this is an opportunity to embrace pain as a minor setback and know that the brief pain is deepening my experience as a human being.

Understandably, as you do this exercise, it might be difficult to believe that simply reframing thoughts from the past that have caused you so much distress will instantly help. Perhaps they feel unchangeable. However, the process of reauthoring your story and changing your inner dialogue might not only deepen your introspection but might open up new avenues of reflection you never imagined.

CHAPTER 3

ACCESSING SPIRITUAL WELL-BEING

The Power of Something Outside Ourselves

*The path of spiritual growth is a
path of lifelong learning.*

M. SCOTT PECK

FOR SO MANY PEOPLE, ESPECIALLY AFTER TRAGIC TIMES, FIND-ing answers to difficult questions is like looking for a needle in a vast field of haystacks. Or worse, looking for a needle in the ocean. In grief therapy, there is no shortage of these questions. *Why did this happen? Why do people have to die? Why is life so cruel sometimes?* Our world has been shaken up, something or someone that was there is no longer, and we are left with existential thoughts and very few answers. We may start to question our very foundations and tightly held belief systems. We may begin to question all that is good and disrupt the delicate emotional buoyancy needed to stay afloat.

However, by accessing some kind of spirituality or faith, you may actually get closer to some of the answers you long for. Or, at the very least, you may get closer to locating one of the haystacks. The English word *spirit* is derived from the Latin *spiritus,* which means to "breathe" or to take in life-giving oxygen. It is literally opening yourself up to life and all its possibility. For many, spirituality connects us to a higher power, which is often a benevolent source. But it can also bring us into harmony with ourselves and others. Whatever that looks like for you, opening yourself up to something bigger than yourself is a key component for building a strong emotional foundation.

While our grief and suffering can cause us to question the universe, see our pain as a kind of punishment, or make us feel incredibly alone, spirituality reminds us that we are all bound by a determinate lifetime and that the universe is on our side. We shift from everything being about our pain and our existential despair to being part of a larger piece of humanity. We pivot from ego-driven individuality to being part of something outside ourselves, from feeling alone to feeling connected.

There's a reason spirituality is one of the cornerstones of the 12-step Alcoholics Anonymous (AA) programs, which for the past ninety years has saved millions of lives, and which I

ACCESSING SPIRITUAL WELL-BEING

am very familiar with as a former drug and alcohol counselor. I saw many individuals who had hit rock-bottom find solace in the ability to "let go, and let God." Letting go of the often egocentric self and ushering in the possibility of a "higher power" or God is a vital tenet of the AA philosophy. This

> SPIRITUALITY JOINS YOU TO OTHERS ASKING THE SAME QUESTIONS.

emotional capitulation allows something else to be in charge. Instead of needing to obsessively control things in your life, you can allow something greater to be of assistance to you. The other healing benefit of the AA community is the inclusive fellowship with other 12-step members who are also trying to access a higher power and locate their own haystacks. Spirituality joins you to others asking the same questions.

Brad Stulberg reported there are science-backed reasons for this spiritual benefit of surrender. "One reason this type of surrender (accepting a higher power) is so effective is that it diminishes activity in a part of the brain called the *posterior cingulate cortex*, or PCC for short. The PCC is a brain region associated with self-referential thinking—science speak for getting caught up in one's own experience."[1] In other words, surrendering to a higher power helps the mind to be less self-absorbed and consider oneself as part of a collective. Instead of being an isolated individual who needs to be strong and independent all the time, spirituality in essence helps us melt away that lone-wolf mentality. It flips the script on the worries and fears that come with navel-gazing and instead draws us into a community of support and compassion. We are not alone. By looking up and looking out, we can retrain our brains to think about something other than ourselves.

Most psychotherapy practices are usually skills-based treatments that adhere to evidence-based protocols. For example, cognitive behavioral therapy helps people restructure their thinking by replacing negative thought patterns with healthier ones. Mindfulness practices help people develop a different relationship with discomfort and teach self-regulation and relaxation techniques (more on mindfulness in a later chapter). But leaning into spirituality affects how we relate to other people, to nature, and to our life purpose. A spiritual life doesn't have to be lofty, but it needs to possess some kind of meaning to motivate us and generate intention, even if temporarily. Whether you're taking care of children, helping others, starting a business, saving up to buy a house, or being creative and sharing your gift with the world, when you align yourself with a sense of spirituality, you increase your awareness of being fully present and gradually attain an attitude of gratitude for all the good that is in the world. You find you are connected to something outside yourself and you have a purpose, a reason for being here.

I suggest that these four pillars of spirituality can help us along the way:

Awareness
Gratitude
Connection
Purpose

ACCESSING SPIRITUAL WELL-BEING

THE VALUE OF AWARENESS

What is *awareness*? It is the ability to observe, feel, and experience our own consciousness. It's a way of knowing ourselves in a more objective way, to see our emotions and even our grief from another perspective—from the outside looking in. In this way of perceiving, we can observe our experience without necessarily comprehending it fully. Awareness is a state of being grounded in the reality of a given moment, but, even more than that, it leads you to notice what you didn't know was already there.

Music can help us tap into awareness. From his play the *Merchant of Venice*, William Shakespeare opined that music could tame the heart of any restless, hot-blooded mortal, "their savage eyes turned to a modest gaze by the sweet power of music."[2]

A more recent example of this, the indie rock group The Flaming Lips sings about the concept of awareness in their 2002 song "Do You Realize?"

Whenever I hear this song, I am overcome with a broad range of mixed feelings. I experience gratitude for the gift of life, but also a sense of the gloomy unavoidability of its finiteness. For a moment, my awareness is expanded. I'm observing, feeling, and experiencing something beyond myself—spirituality via music. The song rhythmically manages to soften the blunt reality of my mortality *and* make me appreciate it at the same time. It's like breathing a happy sigh of surrender—a gentle illustration of how conceding to sadness makes us feel whole.

THE MAGIC IN THE TRAGIC

Sometimes our pain feels like it will last forever, or the sharp grief we experience soon after loss will always feel so acute—but if we can have some awareness of ourselves and the often irrational scenarios we create about our tragedies, we'll be able to separate the reality from the illusion.

ADOPTING AN ATTITUDE OF GRATITUDE

Another cog in the spiritual wheel is developing an attitude of gratitude regardless of what's occurring in the moment and regardless of what's happened to us in the past. Resiliency doesn't come from playing victim and blaming others, or traffic, inflation, or any other obstacle or annoyance. Rather, we can build resiliency through gratitude—actively choosing to refocus every moment of the day.

For me, choosing gratitude is akin to the serenity prayer from Alcoholics Anonymous, which is essentially a mantra to help us focus every day on what we do and don't have control over *and* the wisdom to know the difference. It's also a choice to focus on things in our lives that we still possess, despite the many losses. It's focusing on small gains we have made instead of the failures.

Author Rick Hanson said that adopting an attitude of gratitude includes being thankful in simple ways. He suggested that you "think about what has been fortunate in your life, such as your natural talents ... when or where you were born ... who your parents were."[3] He reminded us to give thanks for things

ACCESSING SPIRITUAL WELL-BEING

we take for granted in nature and in the material world. For myself, the exquisite intricacy of a flower, the shared laughter with friends, my good fortune for having a career that is purposeful, and many more. All of them inspire me. When I pay attention to the good in my life right now, I naturally feel better.

Gratitude helps us make peace with how the events of our life turned out, because we are forever changed by them. As the Greek philosopher Heraclitus observed, no man ever steps in the same river twice, because it's not the same river and he's not the same man.[4]

> GRATITUDE HELPS US MAKE PEACE WITH HOW THE EVENTS OF OUR LIFE TURNED OUT.

This timeless wisdom refers to the ever-changing cycle of life: Just as the water in the river is continually flowing downstream, our lives keep moving. The water we step into in one spot will never be the same water again. Similarly, we can't go back to the past or change the outcome, no matter how much we may want to. We must let it go to some extent, but we can honor and be thankful for how we have changed in the process. If we allow it, our attachment to the past will get washed or carried away by the always evolving and perpetual flow of life. With gratitude, we can accept every day as a brand-new gift and ourselves as new, changed people.

THE NEED FOR HUMAN CONNECTION

Many years ago, I treated a thirty-five-year-old woman named Julie, who was suffering from depression. Julie was a single, well-educated professional who had recently lost her mother to cancer. She reported that after the funeral, she felt a profound sense of isolation. It wasn't so much the bond she had lost with her mother, but more of how alone she felt with her feelings. The rest of her family—two older siblings and an ailing father—all withdrew and coped with the loss in their own private way. Without anyone to share her pain with, Julie began to feel overwhelmed by her sorrow.

In our therapy sessions, Julie began to realize how disconnected she always felt with others and how unacquainted she was with her inner self. Julie had little or no genuine human connection, and as a result, she was quietly suffocating in her unexpressed grief. After working with me for about six months, she began to use our therapeutic connection as a place to safely mourn her departed mother. She also joined a bereavement group with like-minded individuals who had just lost a family member. The entire process changed her life and gave her a strong sense of spiritual belonging.

A few weeks after her treatment ended, she sent me a card with six simple words: "Thank you for giving me oxygen." Julie had found *spiritus* and could finally breathe again.

For the majority of people in the world, experiencing human connection truly feels like receiving oxygen. There is something life-giving when we feel totally understood by someone or when we experience that unique "meeting of the minds." It's so special to us that we've been writing novels, plays, poems, songs, and films about it for centuries. Within the profound bonds of connection, we exchange like-minded

ACCESSING SPIRITUAL WELL-BEING

ideas with one another and build trust. We share joys together, and we grieve together.

As we find strength outside ourselves, human connection is invaluable. Connection ignites the part of the brain that makes us feel good, which subsequently impels us to seek out *more* connection. This has to do with what happens in our brains when we interact with other people. Psychologists have found a strong parallel between social connectedness and reduced anxiety. This is partly because connection can cushion the negative effects of stress. "The brain plays a critical role in coordinating stress responses and encoding social information that may dampen stress responses."[5] The role of supportive human interaction acts like a buffer against psychic pain by decreasing levels of the primary stress hormone, cortisol, and increasing amounts of the feel-good chemical, oxytocin.

The findings also revealed that social connectedness can safeguard individuals from illness as well. It can help fight disease and protect us against other negative health outcomes associated with persistent exposure to adversity and trauma.[6] It appears that human connection is one of the most vital defenses we can access to living a longer life. Care and love from another person are indispensable.

THE POWER OF PURPOSE

A few years ago, I tore a calf muscle in my right leg playing tennis. I was forced to cancel all my patient appointments for a few days. I hobbled on crutches around the house, unable to do very much with myself. By the second day, with my daily purpose and routine temporarily on hold, I felt despondent. Suddenly, I was overmagnifying every apprehension in my life from the basic fear of aging to whether or not I remembered to turn off the air-conditioning before leaving work. It felt like my insides were being gouged out by a new form of human desperation.

Then, self-criticism began to gnaw at me. The usually gratified assessment I possess about my life's work as a psychotherapist disappeared. I was slipping into a cavernous trench of self-doubt. A day later, I realized it was just a temporary detachment from my work, which, for now, is my life purpose. But the gloomy malaise stayed with me for a while.

If every person in the world was temporarily stripped of their daily purpose in life—if they were torn away from their responsibilities and daily routines, like going to work, taking care of children, keeping house, doing laundry—in time there could be global pandemonium. This loss of purpose and structure would create an existential crisis of high anxiety. Most individuals would begin obsessing and worrying about all the wrong things. Idle time for the human mind is worse than the devil's playground; it's the devil's penitentiary. Spirituality helps us find purpose, and we need purpose to function well.

Our life's purpose and the responsibilities of each day, no matter how mundane, help us survive. They prevent us from negatively overthinking about our ephemeral existence. While acquiring awareness is important, we don't want to overdwell on it either.

ACCESSING SPIRITUAL WELL-BEING

If we don't have focus and structure, we tend to look backward more often too. Sometimes with regret. We obsess about mistakes and bad choices with more scrutiny. The despair is liable to creep in and make us dissect the past when we have no business doing so.

That's why the Japanese concept of ikigai, which translates as the happiness in always being busy, is so popular. The state of "flow," a condition of the mind where the individual is so focused on an activity that nothing else is relevant, is the center piece of ikigai. It provides people with a reason to get up in the morning, a reason to live. "Existential frustration arises when our life is without purpose, or when that purpose is skewed," said Hector Garcia and Francesc Miralles, coauthors of *Ikigai: The Japanese Secret to a Long and Happy Life*.[7] Throughout my life, my most productive times have been the happiest times.

ACCESSING SPIRITUALITY THROUGH NATURE AND BEAUTY

Nature and physical beauty also play a big role in generating a sense of spirituality. Nature can help us marvel at the world around us. Its immensity and grandeur allow us to slow down, pull back, and evaluate our purpose.

By appreciating the rustic splendor of a scenic vista overlooking breathtaking mountains or lying on a beach and noticing the deep vastness of the ocean in front of us, we feel

> NATURE HAS A WAY OF GIVING US PERSPECTIVE ... AND FILLING OUR MINDS AND HEARTS WITH APPRECIATION.

connected to something. Nature has a way of giving us perspective, diminishing our mundane problems and the stresses of life that promote fear and worry, and instead filling our minds and hearts with appreciation.

But we need to stop and actually create intention to notice and appreciate nature. Otherwise, we take it for granted. For myself, every time I visit the mystical majesty of Sedona, Arizona, it gives me an enduring source of wonder. The stunning, cathedral-like red sandstone formations and the immense valleys and canyons in between them make my jaw drop. The endless steep-walled rocks and the contrasting pine forests below them impel me to stop and absorb the phenomenon of how such a gorgeous place could have formed on its own. All my senses shift, my central nervous system is redirected, and my heart is softened. And I am filled with awe.

TRY THIS PRACTICE

Accessing Spiritual Well-Being

When we lack spirituality in our lives, we tend to distance ourselves from what's important. We often ignore our feelings, we disconnect from others, we minimize activities that bring us joy, we do things that may be in conflict with our core value system, and we forget to initiate gratitude for what we have. In essence, we lose touch with ourselves.

Try to ask the following questions each morning as a way to stay aligned with your spiritual consciousness.

What am I feeling? Check in with yourself and give yourself compassion for whatever you are feeling. You need to identify emotions in order to soothe your grief.

What am I grateful for today? Name three things in your life that you are thankful for right now. This will help you focus on what you have, not what you don't have.

How am I connecting to others today? Reach out to friends and family on a daily basis. Even if just to say hello. A support system is vital to building emotional resilience.

What am I doing for fun and pleasure? Seek out activities that make you happy and inspire your soul. Play is a big part of staying healthy and balanced. Making daily time for self-care is also crucial.

What is my purpose for today? Align yourself with goals that guide you in the direction you are going, even if they are temporary goals. Behaving consistently with your values gives you purpose.

Keep a reminder of these five questions close to your bed so it's one of the first things you see when you wake up. By establishing an intimate connection with your answers, you are directly summoning spirituality into your life.

CHAPTER 4

HEALTHY ALONENESS

Learning How to Ground Our Emotions

Hello solitude,
how are you today?
Come, sit with me,
And I will care for you.

THICH NHAT HANH

FOR YEARS NOW WE HAVE BEEN LIVING IN AN AGE OF VIRTUAL existence resulting in less in-person relating. The pandemic of 2020 exacerbated this even more with behavioral restrictions like wearing masks, quarantining, and social distancing, which profoundly changed our lifestyles and how we interacted with others. To cooperate with these restrictions, we all had to learn to pull together by pulling apart. Even though the pandemic is in the past, the upheaval it caused on how we interact with others—or don't—still lingers in many ways.

In my experience working as a psychotherapist during that time, I saw many lives negatively disrupted and, in some instances, ruined. I especially witnessed cases where the interruption of people's daily routines—which they depended on in order to function—threw them so out of whack they struggled to recover. Gina, a college student I treated for mild symptoms of anxiety, unexpectedly plunged into a deep hole of depression once her live classes shifted to virtual mode. Despite moving back in with her parents, the lack of appropriate socialization and human interaction with others was debilitating.

And still today, it's difficult for many people to put the pieces back together from that time. The toll on mental health in our country was great, and the principal factor that affected our mental health was the sustained isolation from social distancing and the overall lack of human contact. For an extended time, people were alone or isolated and even touch-deprived, which is not how our species is meant to live, let alone thrive.

Before the pandemic, US surgeon general Dr. Vivek Murthy declared that America was experiencing an epidemic of loneliness. "Loneliness has real consequences to our health and well-being. Being lonely, like other forms of stress, increases the risk of emotional disorders like depression, anxiety and substance abuse."[1] During the pandemic, therapists around the world saw an increase in substance abuse as people tried to cope with loneliness and stress by self-medicating.[2] To add fuel to the fire, the loss of in-person support groups and the shortage of needed medications made it that much harder.

The loss of real, in-person relationships has also affected our physical health. When the brain is exposed to any type of stressor, even isolation, it perceives it as a threat. Consequently, the fight/flight/freeze response mechanism kicks in and a flood of upsetting feelings is activated for the organism to protect itself at any cost. Blood pressure levels rise and inflammation invades the body, which affects the ability to fight infections and viruses.[3] So evolution has always been sending the right signals—protecting us from isolation—but we haven't taken the problems seriously enough.

Murthy also observed that loneliness and the mental health toll "could be driven by the accelerated pace of life and the spread of technology into all of our social interactions. With this acceleration, efficiency and convenience have 'edged out' real relationships."[4] Today, our obsession with screens and social media enables human isolation more than ever. As a society we are consciously detaching from friendships and a sense of community. We have grown comfortable in our own discomfort.

> WE ARE CONSCIOUSLY DETACHING FROM FRIENDSHIPS AND A SENSE OF COMMUNITY.

HEALTHY ALONENESS

So if we know we need people and connection, but we live in a separated, isolated society, what do we do? How do we function and thrive, especially when we experience loss or tragedy?

What if there was a *good* kind of loneliness? A positive alternative to the epidemic kind? I suggest a healthy aloneness could be the solution. Healthy aloneness is when we appreciate the uniqueness of occasionally being alone, instead of panicking about it. It's when we learn to take advantage of our solitude—even though it might make us uncomfortable—and use it for our benefit.

First, it's important to acknowledge that society can feed the notion that if you are alone, it is inherently abnormal. If you are single, unmarried, or unattached to a significant other you may be labeled pejoratively as a "lonely person." But *choosing* to live alone or be unattached is a different issue. There are many who have tried to coexist with others but for whatever reason are better off uncommitted. Close friendships, intimate relationships, and even marriage are not for everyone.

However, for most people, loneliness evokes undesirable emotions, like sadness and alienation. It can feel shameful or taboo. It reveals a disproportionate deficit in human connection that is unsustainable. For some, we feel it even when in the presence of others. Those who have friends, acquaintances, and even spouses can still feel terribly alone. I have treated many high-functioning individuals who live normal lives in society but also feel like outsiders in their own families or with close friends. The physical presence is there but the deep connection needed to feel like they belong is sometimes nonexistent.

When we experience healthy aloneness, we can be alone without feeling lonely. Even if a low-grade sense of sadness is present, it does not debilitate us. Rather, it's more of a conscious awareness that even though we are spatially alone, it's merely a temporary interval of human absence. Big difference. We can prosper in our special alone time. Some people use more acceptable euphemisms like "me time," or in the field of psychotherapy, we actively take some "personal time" or initiate "self-care." Healthy aloneness is prioritizing yourself and your relationship with yourself for a time.

Consequently, there is enormous benefit in knowing the limits of being alone. Despite its restorative quality, humans are not designed for too much of it. We are ultimately made for human connection. And science has shown us that deep in the recesses of our genes, detachment from the bonds that draw us together causes distress. The unease is embedded in our DNA; otherwise, humans would never form those bonds to procreate and survive. Knowing the subtle limits of being apart from other humans, becoming attuned to the discomfort in human separation, is crucial for building emotional resilience.

> WE ARE ULTIMATELY MADE FOR HUMAN CONNECTION.... KNOWING THE SUBTLE LIMITS OF BEING APART FROM OTHER HUMANS IS CRUCIAL.

Some of us embrace our solitude or have developed a

bittersweet relationship with it. Healthy aloneness can temper our emotions and ground the ego. It can allow us to grow more comfortable with the unhappiness and suffering inherent in being human. It opens up space to help us think more clearly, to be more creative, and perhaps to problem-solve. We can also use it for personal reflection and for recharging our mental and physical batteries. If you are someone who can't stand to be alone, you don't need to force yourself into it; but if you are open to it every now and then, you may be surprised where it leads.

GROUNDING OUR EMOTIONS: LONELINESS IN EDWARD HOPPER'S ART

Healthy aloneness can ground our emotions, which is key in building emotional resilience as we face our struggles. When we are grounded in our emotions, it means we understand them better. We've learned to respect them, not fear them.

Exposure to healthy aloneness teaches us that life is difficult and painful but that there is nothing *wrong* with the suffering either. In this case, the *constructive aching* felt around our loneliness is a prerequisite to growing and learning. If we are going to continue changing the discourse on traditional thinking about suffering and discovering alternative ways of facing grief, then let's consider another remarkable artist who can teach us a thing or two about feelings of loneliness.

American painter Edward Hopper has been described

HEALTHY ALONENESS

by art historians as an artist who—like many other artists—suffered a long history of anxiety and depression.[5] He was a shy and reserved man who preferred to relate to people and the world around him from a distance. His way of safely engaging with the world was through his ability to freely and inconspicuously paint. Hopper found a way to ground himself with his introverted art, and his work is a tool for us to ground ourselves as well.

Hopper is best known for his works that depict "urban loneliness"—feelings of isolation one might experience living in a big city despite coexisting with other people. The famed awkward stillness to his paintings has an eerie and evocative quality to it. Yet the tangible detachment also possesses a seductive indifference. The viewer is as much intrigued as they are left feeling cold. Are the paintings intended to be dreamlike or nightmarish? My mind goes back and forth trying to decide. Most of the subjects in his works appear numb, robotic, yet suggestive. Their blank eyes and impervious faces seem arrested in time but still raise our inquiry. Something in his paintings bonds us to them and stimulates a feeling of fascination. What is Hopper trying to convey?

"Behind the apparent simplicity of the paintings lies great complexity and depth. The lack of details invites the spectator to complete the image by speculating on past and impending events, on the relationships between the characters, and on the desires and anxieties provoked by our own need to examine these character's lives."[6] So in being curious about Hopper's characters, we indirectly help ourselves by effectually examining our *own* lives through an artistic lens. For many, the paintings serve as mirrors for our emotions, especially those feelings of loneliness and alienation we see in his subjects. Similar to the impressionistic art movement of the late nineteenth century, where the works were imprecise enough to allow viewers to attach their own subjective feelings to the paintings, in Hopper's work we can see our emotions reflected back to us.

Hopper's most referenced work, the iconic *Nighthawks* (1942), is a perfect example. *Nighthawks* is an evening scene at a local diner, which could be anywhere in America. The characters are frozen in an eerie but passive reverie. They are completely disconnected from one another, yet they are quietly curious about one another too. The scene of inner-city desolation is profound and mesmerizing at the same time.

We can learn much from his artwork. Loneliness portrayed via the compelling world of an Edward Hopper painting is Exposure Therapy 101—a common therapeutic technique that, in small doses, exposes people to activities and situations they fear. By witnessing his work, we can become comfortable with loneliness by soaking ourselves in it. Over time, it can meaningfully ground us. Just as we observe the emotions in the painting, we can become observers of our own loneliness (we see ourselves objectively, as if on canvas) instead of casualties of it. British writer, novelist, and cultural critic Olivia Laing offered up a thorough, in-depth analysis of Hopper's work. "Edward Hopper's haunting painting can make us feel less alone. And yet what Hopper captures is beautiful as well as frightening. As if loneliness was something worth looking at. More than that, as if looking itself was an antidote, a way to defeat loneliness's estranging spell."[7]

By exposing ourselves to loneliness through art we can alter the "estranging spell" it has over us. If we pay more attention to the inspiration that moves us so acutely, we can create the right kind of intention for it to change our perspective, fill in the gaps, and give words to the unspoken inner workings of our psyche. We can find purpose and become better aware of our place in the greater collective. We can evolve from our debilitating loneliness to a healthy aloneness that we can make sense of.

GOVERNED BY EMOTIONS: WHEN LONELINESS FEELS LIKE EMPTINESS

While immersing ourselves in art that can help us grow more comfortable with healthy aloneness, we also want to be cautious of where feelings of loneliness can take us. One of the problems with prolonged exposure to loneliness is that it can cause symptoms of depression. These "down in the dumps" episodes often trick our minds into thinking we are hopelessly alone and there is little to live for. As a result, we think our lives are devoid of meaning. We feel empty inside.

Yet one of the most important techniques to managing depression is comprehending that the feeling of depression itself skews our thoughts—not the events that have triggered the depression. It makes us see the world within the narrow confines of our dark thoughts. Subsequently, negative thoughts influence our emotions, and we fall into the emotional reasoning trap.

Emotional reasoning is when we are unaware that we view ourselves, the world, and the future based on how our emotions are governing us. Our thoughts become dangerously twisted and we default into reality distortion:

> *If I feel lonely, it must mean I am unwanted.*
> *If I feel scared, it must mean I am in danger.*
> *If I feel sad, it must mean life is pointless.*

It's no longer our situation that depresses us but rather the negative thoughts in the moment generated by the depression. There is some *magic in the tragic* in knowing this possibility, because if you can separate the negative thought from reality and you can notice the difference between perception and distortion, you will feel more in control of your emotions. In the midst of our pain, we don't always think so well. We are easily governed by our emotions and sometimes need to step back to see what's really going on.

> *I feel lonely, but that doesn't mean I'm unwanted.*
> *I feel scared, but that doesn't mean I'm in danger.*
> *I feel sad, but that doesn't mean my life is pointless.*

Pain often gets a bad rap. Naturally, we want to avoid it.

But pain can actually be your travel partner instead of your enemy. Perhaps a reluctant co-passenger in this life journey, an entity to join forces with instead of resisting. Similarly, healthy aloneness can really be your friend. You don't have to fear it or resist it.

When we address that feeling of emptiness that can come with being alone, we lift up the soul and ultimately pay homage to our pain. Author and philanthropist Sheryl Sandberg wrote, "When tragedy occurs . . . you can give in to the void . . . Or you can try to find meaning."[8] You can choose how to approach or give in to your pain—as an overwhelming obstacle or something imbued with meaning. The reverence you assign to it and the respect you offer it could be the beginning of a new and beautiful friendship. At first, this may not be possible in your deepest stages of grief or after overwhelming loss, but little by little you can reframe your pain and loss as something that carries purpose.

REFRAMING LONELINESS

Many years ago, I treated a patient in my private practice who was going through a late midlife crisis. Brent was a moderately successful businessman who was pushing fifty-five. He had been divorced for many years with two grown children. Then, after a bitter breakup and some business setbacks that caused him financial hardship, he began to withdraw from his usually active social life. For the first time, he became terribly disconnected from the world. His depression and despair caused him to isolate against his better judgment. His self-esteem plummeted and he felt a profound sense of emptiness in his life. His entire life shrank down to the size of a postage stamp. He was falling into a deep hole. He never shared these feelings with his children or his friends because he didn't want to impose.

In our sessions, the more we processed his empty feelings, the more he learned that his depression was not necessarily related to feeling lonely but was more about what he made *being alone* mean. To him, it meant he was a failure of some kind—a pathetic little man with no one to love and be loved by. He realized that he harbored shameful feelings about being unattached. His traditional European parents and extended family all remained paired up until old age, and divorce and singlehood were not encouraged in his culture. The core belief he held was that if he was alone, something must be wrong with him. Or he was a failure.

However, once he began reframing his negative perception, things changed. He started to realize that for most of his adult life he had never had *any* time to himself. His entire adult life was abidingly dedicated to his children, his career, and his extended family. So as he started to embrace his involuntary downtime, he began appreciating new things, like reading a good book, listening to his favorite music, playing golf and tennis, watching movies, and going out in nature. Brent finally started to find value and inspiration outside of his work, and outside of being a father or a good partner to somebody. He discovered there could be beauty in his life even if he was alone. Suddenly "healthy aloneness" took over his fear of loneliness and the shame of being unattached.

Brent's discovery not only motivated him to engage in new activities and possibilities in his life, which were always there but rarely accessed, but it also caused him to reevaluate the way he had been living his life. He began to choose different partners, to exercise more self-compassion, to embark on a spiritual journey to give his life new meaning. All things he had never done before. In a sense, he was reborn out of his loneliness (and through therapy), learning to coexist with his unasked-for single status in life and transform it into healing and discovery. Healthy aloneness became a heartening agent, something to move him forward rather than something to be ashamed of. This shift, this new lease on life, may have never occurred without the emotional crisis he suffered. Sometimes when things feel like they are falling apart, they are actually falling into their rightful place.

> HEALTHY ALONENESS CAN BE A HEARTENING AGENT, SOMETHING TO MOVE YOU FORWARD.

TRY THIS PRACTICE

Practicing Healthy Aloneness

The first phase in learning to coexist with loneliness is acknowledgment. Instead of yielding to your knee-jerk reaction to fight loneliness, admit your loneliness. Accept that it's causing you discomfort in the moment. By reframing your loneliness as healthy aloneness, you alter its negative association. For example, say to yourself, *Just because I am physically alone right now does not mean something is wrong.*

To help you come up with a new response to your loneliness, consider the disquieting feelings you experience as beautiful *and* poignant. Discover the value of occasional exposure to loneliness.

It's obviously not advisable to wait for your most distressing moments of loneliness to perform this exercise. My former patient Brent had to reach rock-bottom to find his way up and out, but that does not have to be the case for you. You can assign some healthy aloneness time for yourself as a regular practice, and I would suggest a brief time, no more than five minutes a day.

By intentionally assigning and planning healthy aloneness time—rather than waiting for an upsetting event to catch you by surprise—you can take control of your feelings. The practice will help you master your reaction for when the unexpected does come. The goal is to transform the reflexive reaction to the pain of loneliness into a grateful posture of being by yourself.

Step 1. Assign a five-minute "loneliness exposure" time. Find a quiet place in your home. Sit comfortably in a chair or sofa. Or lie down on a yoga mat or even on your bed.

Step 2. Acknowledge your loneliness. Take a few deep breaths and admit that right now you are physically alone and you might be feeling uncomfortably isolated.

Step 3. Recite "healthy aloneness" affirmations. Try some of the affirmations below, or write your own. Whisper them or quietly recite them in your mind. You may need to repeat the affirmations several times.

- *What I am feeling right now is not negative loneliness, but healthy aloneness.*
- *To build emotional resilience, I need to experience uncomfortable feelings without fighting them.*
- *Healthy aloneness is important "me time." It allows me to check in with myself and do a mental reset.*
- *For now, I choose to focus on the instructive power of healthy aloneness.*
- *Healthy aloneness will bring me closer to others and make me feel less afraid of being by myself.*
- *It's okay for me to be unattached and not in a relationship.*
- *I am not a failure if I am single.*
- *I choose to see the value in temporarily feeling alone.*
- *I choose to focus on the grounding, poetic language of momentary melancholy.*

- *My loneliness now may be making space for new possibilities.*

Be prepared to experience some pushback from your natural inclination to avoid spending time alone. But each time you do it, you raise your distress tolerance levels and build resilience.

CHAPTER 5

FINDING THE OPTIMISM IN DEPRESSION

An Uninvited Catalyst

*The biggest emotion in creation
is the bridge to optimism.*

SIR BRIAN MAY

IN 2022 THE AMERICAN PSYCHIATRIC ASSOCIATION ADDED A new disorder to its Diagnostic and Statistical Manual of Mental Health Disorders (DSM-5 TR)—prolonged grief disorder.[1] While grief and death have always been with us, in the pandemic the whole world encountered loss of life on such a scale, under such unusual and jarring circumstances, and often without adequate ways of processing and grieving, that it required a new classification.

Prolonged grief is not a new condition. What *is* new is the research: Decades of research has found that severity and duration of symptoms for individuals experiencing bereavement-related struggles exceeded what is typically expected in our society and culture. The pandemic revealed on a large scale that the world was already grieving—and for longer periods than ever before. It's no wonder we have officially ushered in a new age of depression and persistent grief.

What do we do? How do we face the mental health crisis we are in? In our efforts to reframe grief and build emotional resilience, it can help us to understand prolonged grief and depression better—and maybe even find a catalyst for growth and change.

WHAT IS PROLONGED GRIEF DISORDER (PGD)?

According to the American Psychological Association (APA), prolonged grief disorder (PGD) happens when someone experiences a great deal of personal loss and then has an intense yearning, longing for, or preoccupation with the deceased person that lasts for an extended amount of time, and with persistent grief responses that occur most of the day, nearly every day, for at least the last month before getting diagnosed.[2] Their bereavement lasts longer than social norms suggest and the resulting distress profoundly interferes with important activities of daily living. Typically, prolonged grief disorder happens when the deceased has been dead for at least twelve months (for adults) or six months (for children and adolescents).

Prolonged grief causes people to be "fixed" in mourning and live in a protracted state of despondency. It's more than just grief; it's a state of consciousness that twists perceptions of reality and diminishes the ability to hope. The person feels like they're being wedged in a tight corner of continual sorrow and rumination. These extended episodes can lead to severe bouts of despair and dysfunction. And it's not just a problem for those who are more prone to depression. Even people who have been seemingly untouched by depression throughout their lives are feeling it these days.

Some symptoms of prolonged grief disorder:[3]

- Identity disruption (e.g., feeling as though part of oneself has died)
- Marked sense of disbelief about the death
- Avoidance of reminders that the person is dead
- Intense emotional pain (e.g., anger, bitterness, sorrow) related to the death
- Difficulty with reintegration (e.g., problems engaging with friends, pursuing interests, planning for the future)
- Emotional numbness
- Feeling that life is meaningless
- Intense loneliness (i.e., feeling alone or detached from others)

As you can see from this list, the fallout of extended grief has enormous effects on the psychological, emotional, and social well-being of a person. The grief experienced is deeply personal and disruptive to the person's psyche, but it can also change how that person functions (or doesn't) with others and in society. For instance, prolonged grief can cause individuals to isolate from their friends and from members of their community. In some instances, it can even cause them to withdraw from the essential, intimate relationships they need most.

In reality, all people experience some symptoms of depression throughout their lives in varying degrees. Sometimes these symptoms are what we call the everyday "blues," and other times they can be more serious. There are also circumstantial or incidental cases of depression that are due to a specific event or occurrence such as a death, trauma, chronic illness, relationship problem, or a natural disaster like an earthquake, tsunami, flood, wildfire, and the like. If these tough times begin to interfere with your ability to function on a day-to-day basis, or you've noticed changes in your temperament—like mood swings, a negative outlook on life, or a persistent bad temper—it may be depression.

WHAT IS DEPRESSION?

Depression—as opposed to mild, everyday ups and downs—is when an individual's symptoms are so acute that they affect their ability to function in life. For example, if an individual's basic, everyday routines are negatively affected and cannot be completed, or if the individual is unable to fulfill major role obligations such as going to work or school, or taking care of children and family, this may be depression. For an individual to be diagnosed with serious depression, they must be experiencing some of the following symptoms, which will have been present for two weeks or more:[4]

- Feelings of hopelessness
- Sadness or low mood (sometimes suicidal thoughts)
- Loss of interest in things that usually give pleasure
- Poor concentration
- Irritability or restlessness
- Fatigue
- Loss of appetite (or overeating)
- Insomnia (or oversleeping)
- Feelings of guilt

Depression is the second most common mental illness in the United States, second only to anxiety.[5] In 2023 nearly 29 percent of Americans reported having been diagnosed with a major depression episode at some point in their lives, an increase of 10 percent since 2015.[6] Future projections estimate that depression will be the second leading cause of disability throughout the world, trailing only heart disease.[7] But the good news is that depression is a treatable condition, which, if identified early, can be prevented from getting worse.

THE MAGIC IN THE TRAGIC

WHY DO PEOPLE GET DEPRESSED?

There are many reasons why people suffer from depression. Some people are born with a genetic predisposition to it. Others experience depression later in life, often as a result of environmental factors, a traumatic circumstance, or a series of events that kindle the fire of the brain's genetic tendencies. Whatever the cause, depression is affected by chemical changes in the brain, specifically with certain neurotransmitters that are most vital for regulating mood, like serotonin, norepinephrine, and dopamine.

When we are in the grips of a depressive episode, unbeknownst to us, we experience a malfunction in the brain. The chemical messengers, the critical neurotransmitters that help to regulate mood and affect, are not firing correctly. And the decreased brain activity in the hippocampus leads to negative emotions and the loss of cognitive processing and rational thinking. The neurotransmitter serotonin is responsible for controlling essential bodily functions like sleeping, eating, sexual activity, and regulating emotions. So if there is a decrease in production of serotonin, that could cause symptoms of depression. Another neurotransmitter, dopamine, plays an important role in controlling a person's drive to seek out reward, pleasure, and soothing. When people are depressed, they often don't find pleasure in social interactions and in doing things they usually enjoy—also known as anhedonia—which can be the result of low dopamine.

Depression can also manifest in less obvious symptomatic

ways: for example, as irritability, impatience, edginess, getting upset easily, or a general apathy about life. These symptoms may not mean a person is depressed, but many people out there don't realize they are mildly depressed and may blow off these symptoms and never address them.

Regardless of its origin, when depression gets serious and severe symptoms appear consistently and have for an extended period, it's considered "clinical depression." Clinical depression is when an individual's symptoms are so acute and so severe that their life is significantly impaired, and they need professional care and possibly medication or other forms of treatment.

Depression is considered an illness of the brain, but unlike other physical illnesses or even a brain injury, we can't see the injury in the same way with external symptoms. Some people with high-functioning depression may not exhibit obvious symptoms, even to the people closest to them. These people may be good at masking and hiding how they feel while inwardly they are grappling with great pain. The more we can do to understand depression and remove the stigmas around mental health issues, the better off we will be.

> THE MORE WE CAN DO TO UNDERSTAND DEPRESSION AND REMOVE THE STIGMAS AROUND MENTAL HEALTH ISSUES, THE BETTER OFF WE WILL BE.

THE HIGHS AND LOWS OF LIVING WITH DEPRESSION

One of the most intriguing public figures of our time who suffered severe bouts of depression was President Abraham

THE MAGIC IN THE TRAGIC

Lincoln. Granted, it's not easy to posthumously diagnose someone who lived more than a century ago, but according to letters written to his wife and several close friends and confidants, Lincoln was a man prewired for despondency.[8]

Lincoln's formative years were severely affected by not only the passing of his mother but also a complicated relationship with his cold and cruel father. Even after his mother died, his father, Thomas, left him and his sister for long periods of time unaccompanied while he went looking for a new wife. Lincoln's father, illiterate and socially unpolished, often beat his son for choosing to read books instead of completing chores. The relationship was so strained and acrimonious that Abraham did not visit his father at his deathbed and refused to attend his funeral.[9] Lincoln's potentially predisposed psyche coupled with the trauma of his mother's death and father's mistreatment may have sealed his psychological fate.

But even though these events left him susceptible to depression, there were obviously periods of time when Lincoln had clarity of mind and was able to accomplish so much, like presiding over a country in turmoil, fighting a brutal civil war, and ending slavery. How was he able to accomplish so much while dealing with a mental health condition? Depression is not always static or debilitating. "Depression does not have to be incapacitating to qualify as depression. The key feature of the condition is that these episodes can come and go. It does not plague people every minute of the day," explained author Claudia Kalb in her book *Andy Warhol Was a Hoarder*.[10] Lincoln was able to manage his condition and accomplish great things in spite of his depression. He might be the most accomplished high-functioning depressive in history.

But you don't have to be considered the greatest US president of all time or a legendary public figure to hold the tension of having both periods of mental health distress and periods of stability and euphoria. Many of us understand the reality of our depressive moods and our capacity to be productive in our lives. For example, as a writer, there are times I think my work has value and other times it feels like I couldn't write a grocery list.

If you find yourself drifting between these places of instability and stability, from apathy to productivity, know that you aren't alone. Make the most of your high times, and when you're in a low time, know it won't last forever. In addition, kindly remind yourself not to believe every depressed thought you think. Sometimes thoughts are just thoughts and don't have much validity in the moment.

DEPRESSION AS A CATALYST

Some people can be productive in spite of their depression; others *because* of it. Depression can be a catalyst, boosting some people to achieve great acts even in their more dreadful states because they fear the incapacitating effects of despair. In times of crisis, maybe the despair is pivotal in making tough decisions in an expedient manner.[11]

Could depression make people better leaders, writers,

philosophers, and composers? Is there optimism to be found in our epidemic of depression? American poet Emily Dickinson said, "People need hard times and oppression to develop psychic muscles." Sometimes opportunity and growth are disguised as hardship. Hence, perseverance and grit in the face of insurmountable odds can be a propitious friend. Depression can be the ultimate motivator and the mother of invention.

Winston Churchill called his depression the "black dog," and he often self-medicated with daily intakes of whiskey and champagne. He will always be remembered as the World War II hero that saved England from the Nazis and helped preserve democracy in Europe. But "although some acknowledge that he had mental problems, few appreciate the relevance of those problems to his prodigious leadership abilities," wrote Nassir Ghaemi in his book *A First-Rate Madness*.[12] Could Churchill's depression have played more of an important role by intensifying his recognition of the dangers posed by the Nazis and thus prompting him to stand up to adversity? Could it be that some mental illnesses amplify crisis management, even on a global war stage? Perhaps his "black dog" deserves more credit.

Ghaemi pointed out that Dr. Martin Luther King Jr. and Mahatma Gandhi also appear to have had a history of depression, which shaped them and their legacies. Both displayed what appear to be acute bouts of high-functioning depression, which may have generated their leadership roles and galvanized their politics of fundamental empathy. They both possessed transformative powers of empathy that probably came from a lifetime of despair and sadness. Gandhi was notably shy and anxious as well. He was susceptible to significant mood swings and often plunged into dark periods of pessimism.[13]

Yet Gandhi said, "Joy lies in the fight, in the attempt in the suffering involved, not in the victory itself."[14] Gandhi's deep understanding of suffering and his great empathy for those who also suffer was a game changer. By decisively implementing his own visceral pain into his teachings, he inspired millions of people. We can glean a sense of optimism in what his inner struggles with depression positively developed in him.

> "JOY LIES IN THE FIGHT, IN THE ATTEMPT IN THE SUFFERING INVOLVED, NOT IN THE VICTORY ITSELF."

Like Lincoln, it appears that Martin Luther King Jr. dealt with an inconstant depression marked by episodic spells of mania and brilliance. Although King was not a believer in the science of psychology and always refused treatment, he was aware of his proclivity to distress and worry. He once stated, "Human salvation lies in the hands of the creatively maladjusted."[15] Even though King is talking about fervidly standing up to injustice via peaceful nonconformity, he may also be telling us that sometimes, unorthodox thinking and acts of radical ingenuity are needed to survive. In other words, an even-keeled mind is not always a fertile mind.

Before depression was given a diagnostic categorization, legend has it that ancient Greek philosophers called *melancholia* the "affliction of geniuses." They saw the upside to sadness as being the impetus for fueling literary and artistic creation. They believed that many of the great works of art could only be born from the enlightening and catalytic result of human suffering. These days, the psychological or philosophical benefits of suffering have been greatly diminished.

DEPRESSION IS NOT A CHOICE

As a boy, the comments I endured about my mental health issues were always confusing to me. Whenever I heard well-intentioned platitudes such as, "Don't worry about it! What are you so anxious about? You don't look depressed," I often felt worse. Not because I found the oversimplification of my feelings to be insensitive, but because even though it sounded logical enough to have the ability to alter my mood on my own, I couldn't make myself feel better. As a result, I felt even more helpless because if I did not have the willpower to stabilize myself, surely I was a weak person. Sadly, for a long time I thought I was the only one who felt this way.

Years later I fell into a deep episode of depression that knocked me flat on my back. We've all heard the clichés that dentists get cavities, bankers go bankrupt, and your average, garden-variety psychotherapist suffers from mental health issues too. Fair enough. However, this was different. This time it was the big "D." That menacing ten-letter word that carries so much shame and stigma that no one likes to admit having it, let alone talk about it. Navy blue days, ebony black nights—and every dark shade in the Crayola box. And I was the furthest thing from a high-functioning depressive. I was

FINDING THE OPTIMISM IN DEPRESSION

like Lincoln in his most wretched days, except minus the brilliant mind, strong will, huge vitality, and all the incredible accomplishments he's known for.

Like many kids, my childhood was chaotic and inconsistent. Sometimes it was harsh. I often escaped reality by indulging my beleaguered senses with music and by plunging headfirst into the unlimited fantasies of motion pictures. They always delivered.

One evening during that murky interlude of depression, I rewatched the 1957 Western *Gunfight at the O.K. Corral* with Kirk Douglas and Burt Lancaster. Douglas plays Doc Holliday, an ex-doctor, gunslinger, and avid gambler who is slowly dying from tuberculosis. There is a memorable scene when Holliday is playing poker at a saloon. At the same time, a gang of rough riders is shooting up the town. You can hear gunshots and people screaming and yelling outside. Bullets fly past Holliday, shattering lamps and liquor bottles and boring holes in the walls of the saloon. But he doesn't flinch, blink, or move a muscle despite the blizzard of lead whizzing by his head. He looks up at the terrified card dealer (who naturally wants to end the game and take cover) and says unaffectedly, "Just keep dealing. I'm not breaking this run. Hit me!"[16]

I was always in awe of Holliday's bravery, his coolness in the face of danger. But this time, something occurred to me. The guy had tuberculosis. He knew he was going to die. That's why he chose not to move. Depression can be similar. When it's acute you don't care what happens to you.

Another character who is desperate and suffering from

an incurable disease is Walter White in the television series *Breaking Bad*. White, played by actor Bryan Cranston, magnanimously chooses to make sure his family is taken care of financially before he dies from terminal lung cancer. Granted, he chooses a life of crime, which I am not condoning, but he is oblivious to the consequences of the law, just as Doc Holliday is oblivious to the bullets.

Both characters have the ability to choose. But when you're depressed, you don't always get to choose—depression chooses for you.

I realize now why I've always related to characters who have nothing to lose. Besides decreasing my depression and feeling moved by their self-sacrifice, it also makes me feel less alone when I put myself in their shoes. They are like family to me. The truth is, until you experience severe depression yourself, until you know what it's like to not care if you get hit by a bullet or stricken with a fatal illness, the reality of depression is too hard for the inexperienced mind to grasp.

For example, the word *depression* was an import to my immigrant parents. In the era they were raised—the 1930s and 1940s—the words *depression* and *anxiety* did not exist as they do today. "Mental illness" was assigned to psychotic people isolated in padded white rooms wearing straitjackets. So, as a child, in the rare instances I *did* opt to share my mental distress with my father, he often replied with a well-intentioned line that was genuinely meant to toughen me up. He would say pointedly: "When I was your age, I held three jobs!" Or he would remind me: "You have a roof over your head, clothes to wear, and plenty of food to eat. So, there's nothing to be sad about." My father was genuinely trying to help me.

I respected, loved, and feared my father all at the same time. I believed every word he said. If he told me there was cheese on the mountain, you better believe I was bringing crackers. But I quickly learned to be intolerant of my feelings. I started believing that depressed people, including myself, simply wanted attention. Or worse, to escape accountability. In other words, I believed depression was a choice.

Although I'm not Doc Holliday or Walter White, thankfully, or anyone else with nothing to lose, I can still commiserate with the utter desperation, because in my times of depression I feel I have *everything* to lose. And when I say desperation, I don't mean just feeling hopeless; I mean the existential dread of having temporarily lost your desire to live and not knowing how to get it back even if you are not dying of an incurable illness. But it's the commitment to seeing the dignity in my pain and embracing my constructive aching and positive wounding that makes the difference. I need to stay plugged in to the inspiring vibrations of my coveted examples of fine art, music, literature, poetry, movies, and touching stories like Abraham Lincoln's struggle with his chronic sadness.

The following exercise will help ease some of the grief you may have hardened against over the years. It may assist in helping you find optimism in your past sorrows.

TRY THIS PRACTICE

Write Yourself a Sympathy Card or Letter

In this exercise, write a sympathy card or, better yet, a short sympathy letter to yourself. It doesn't have to be about someone close to you who has died. It could be a sympathy card or letter about any significant loss in your life. It could be about a past relationship that didn't work out, a missed career opportunity, a major disappointment, a failed business venture, a trauma that you went through as a child, or it could be almost any grievous occurrence that you feel is still negatively affecting you.

In the card or letter, offer yourself condolences for the loss and all the pain the unfortunate event(s) caused you. Give yourself permission to be sad and tell yourself to take all the time you need to grieve. Give yourself the kind of compassionate attention that you know you deserve without offering solutions or suggestions. Honor yourself with the kind of unconditional loving support that will inevitably help you to heal. Remember, the only antidote to grief is in the grieving.

Keep the card or letter handy and read it to yourself whenever you are feeling overwhelmed with any upset(s) from the past. When you reread it, listen to the words, and pay attention to your feelings. Turn the ache in your heart into something epic and grand. Dignify the pain and be proud of your wound.

CHAPTER 6

WHY WE WORRY

Seeing Anxiety as an Asset

*The misfortunes hardest to bear
are those which never come.*
JAMES RUSSELL LOWELL

HOW MUCH TIME DO YOU SPEND WORRYING ABOUT THINGS THAT will never happen? Or worrying more than is necessary? Does worrying ever get you anywhere? Nobody likes uncertainty, or at least the kind that puts us or our loved ones in danger. Not knowing what's coming can make us feel out of control. It rattles our sense of safety and security and leaves us waiting for the other shoe to drop.

Worry is no exception, and it's here to stay. Worry is a state of unease that causes us to dwell on immediate or future uncertainties, sometimes with compulsive persistence. Worry

> WORRY HELPS US PRIORITIZE AND PROTECT THE THINGS THAT ARE IMPORTANT IN OUR LIVES.

can be all-consuming and exhausting, because we obsess, we ruminate, we spin, we loop. It can easily snowball into something unrecognizable from its origins. It compels us to overestimate danger and underestimate our ability to cope with it.

But is it always a bad thing? We often see it as something negative, something we should try to avoid. But worry is our mind's way of protecting us from harm and perpetuating our existence. There's an evolutionary value to many of our unpleasant emotions, so we can thank those cave-dwelling ancestors of ours. Worry protects us, and anxiety can propel us forward. If we didn't worry about things, we probably would have been hit by a car a long time ago because we wouldn't have looked both ways. Or we never would have gone to the doctor when we felt sick. Or we'd be terrible at our jobs and get fired. Or we'd be reckless and neglectful parents. Worry helps us prioritize and protect the things that are important in our lives.

Our world is full of uncertainties, and this is unlikely to change anytime soon, but we can shift the way we think about worry, anxiety, and stress to build emotional resilience despite the uncertainty. We all know the negative effects of stress. It makes us less productive and affects our emotional health. It also weakens the immune system and makes us more susceptible to viruses and other illnesses. When we are anxious, the stress hormone cortisol and other hormones are increased in the brain, which suppresses the immune system.[1]

But we can work on our antianxiety coping skills and monitor and manage our persistent worries. We don't need to try and abolish them. Extinction is not the goal here.

When worry starts to become excessive, it takes away from being present in our lives.

Our mind says:

If I worry enough about something, bad things won't happen.
If I stay vigilant all the time, I will be safer.

But what if "worrying enough" and "being vigilant all the time" take over our lives? There's a big difference between protecting and helping—and keeping us from living our lives.

What is the specific benefit we get from worry? Why do we do it so much? To answer those questions, we need to go back to the concept of uncertainty. Human beings are very attached to feeling good and very averse to feeling bad. Uncertainty makes us feel bad—really bad. In order to soothe the fear of uncertainty, we engage in thinking patterns that create the illusion of safety, but in the end, they cause us more distress. Science tells us that the brain has a keen ability to adapt and rewire itself, known as neuroplasticity.[2] Our central nervous system can alter its activity in response to stimuli and form new neural pathways by restructuring synaptic connections, especially ones responsible for learning. In other words, we can actively change our brain. So if our constant need to worry is caused by negative thinking patterns from the abstracts we employ to help ease our fears, we can actively change those patterns and worry less.

THE PROBLEM WITH FIXED THINKING

Tyler was a twenty-four-year-old law school student suffering from moderate to severe anxiety. He worked part-time as a personal assistant to an attorney in downtown Los Angeles. He was bright and ambitious, but he often mistook intuitive thoughts for ironclad truths. Fixed thinking made him believe that his first instincts were reliable barometers for every stressful situation. By "fixed thinking," I mean when we engage in thinking patterns so consistently that they gradually become our organizing principles, which are personal beliefs, interpretations, and conclusions we have established in our minds to protect us from imagined harm, failure, and rejection from others.

Six months earlier, Tyler had lost his forty-nine-year-old father to cancer. They were very close, and Tyler always looked to him for guidance. Without his father's sage advice, his confidence level dropped and his anxiety increased. His chronic worry impaired his ability to grieve his father's passing because he was afraid to fail and somehow tarnish his father's legacy.

Whenever Tyler worried about something, he was unaware that he was unduly heeding the absolutism of his first impressions. If his boss didn't smile at him in the morning, he immediately concluded he was going to get fired by the end of the week. If his girlfriend was having a bad day and was not particularly attentive to him, he instantly feared she was angling to break up with him.

Tyler avoided people, places, and events in case something went wrong because his initial fear was misinterpreted as trustworthy foresight. But it was actually anxiety he was experiencing and an instinctive attachment to his fixed thinking.

After many weeks of psychotherapy and learning how initial responses to fear are usually exaggerated reflexes intended to protect us, he began to pivot in his relationship to worry. He began to slow down his maladaptive fear-assessment process and became more reflective than reactive.

In the end, my treatment with him had little to do with ignoring his intuition but, instead, challenging his automatic thoughts. Tyler also had to uncheck the "fixed thinking" box in his mind that previously concluded that he couldn't make sound decisions without his late father's counsel. As a result, his anxiety decreased, and he was finally able to appropriately mourn his father's transition.

The mental health treatment modality of cognitive behavioral therapy, a type of psychotherapy that helps people recognize and ultimately restructure their negative thinking and behavior patterns, has identified many fixed thinking templates that promote stress. Even though these templates operate automatically and sometimes unconsciously, they drive our existence and dominate all our human interactions and experiences. At times they even obscure reality and blind us to the truth.

For example, someone may have an *organizing principle* that after a loss or a tragedy, if you grieve for too long, you will suffer more. And that the best way to heal from a tragedy is to never talk about it, or somehow erase it from your memory.

Here are three of the most popular types of fixed thinking patterns that cause distress.

1. Excessive Need for Control

We develop an aversion to uncertainty, and we chronically grasp for guarantees in a world that has *zero* guarantees. We want to always know the outcome of everything. Our motto is: *If I don't have control, I will lose everything that's important to me.* But the need for excessive control makes us feel more stressed and "out of control" because the actual attempt to gain control often fails. It creates a vicious cycle that can never be resolved. It's like watching the 1997 James Cameron film *Titanic* over and over again hoping the ship won't sink the next time. The ship *always* sinks.

2. Perfectionism

We see things in absolute, all-or-nothing terms. For example: *If I don't ace this test,* or *If I don't get that promotion at work, I will always be a failure and I will never be respected by my peers.* In other words, we succeed at 100 percent, but we fail at 98 percent. Perfectionism locks us into seeing ourselves and the world around us in limited ways. It resides in the tipping point of constant, imagined disaster. Perfectionism also impedes our growth and robs us of happiness. When we are so focused on being perfect or having things be a certain way, we aren't open to organically learning via our mistakes. As a result, we deprive ourselves of potentially amazing experiences and miss out on what could make us happy. In *Hidden Potential*, Adam Grant defined it masterfully: "If perfectionism were a medication, the label would alert us to common side effects. *Warning: may cause stunted growth.* Perfectionism traps us in a spiral of tunnel vision and error avoidance."[3]

3. Relying on Others for Approval

This is also known as "people pleasing." We want everyone to like us. We fear disappointing anyone, and as a result, we engage in apologetic behavior in order to not be rejected. It makes us dependent on the reactions and opinions of others regarding what we say, how we look, and how we perform in life. It's a recipe for anxiety because over time, we develop a pseudoself that lives and dies by how we think others are perceiving us and creates in us a deep-seated fear of inadequacy. But like excessive need for control and perfectionism, people pleasing is a habit that can be broken.

All three of these thinking styles are psychological defense mechanisms against illusory disasters, and those mechanisms have actually brought us good results in the past. We keep doing them for good reason. They are adaptive functions that have helped us survive in a world that sometimes feels topsy-turvy. They help us be more goal-oriented and keep good attention to detail. They make us more responsible, and they also help us be social and kind. They prepare us for future seismic shifts that can send our compasses spinning. But these functions can also be examples of overadaptation. Meaning, we can be hyperresponsible and even hyperfearful for the purpose of self-preservation. If not monitored properly, control, perfectionism, and people pleasing can twist our reality and take over our lives.

How can we learn to let go of potentially harmful ways of thinking? What if the knee-jerk reaction of negativity could be metamorphosized into something inspiring? What if our fixed thinking could be a benefit instead of a hindrance? What if we can convert emotional breakdowns into breakthroughs?

CHANGING HOW WE THINK: MAGRITTE'S EXAMPLE FROM ART

As we consider how our fixed thoughts can obscure our reality, we can look at the surrealistic paintings of Belgian artist René Magritte and how his artwork stimulates the mind to think twice about what we take for granted.

René Magritte was a reserved and private artist who connected with his audience almost exclusively through his works. Magritte enjoyed challenging the automatic and habitual reactions to everyday things. Although he's best known for his self-portraits wearing his signature bowler hat and dark suit, the majority of his paintings are shrewd conundrums for us to contemplate. In *The Essential René Magritte,* Todd Alden's analysis of the artist is spot-on: "A paradox-loving master of contradiction, Magritte is the Confucius of Confusion."[4]

In 1934 Magritte painted four artworks called *The Human Condition*. The series of paintings, *La condition humaine* in French, are at first glance mystifying to understand. But when we pause and look closely, his intention becomes clearer. One of Magritte's most common artistic devices was to hide objects behind other objects. Magritte used recognizable images, and then altered them into enigmatic and unfamiliar things. In life, there are things we cannot see because our tightly bolted beliefs hide them from us until someone or something shows us otherwise.

In one of the paintings from the series, Magritte presents a window scene in an average house looking out into a pastoral vista. It's a tranquil landscape with a lone tree standing tall in a field of grass. But when you zoom into the painting, you see that there's a canvas resting on a wooden easel that is precisely framed to fit the window. The canvas is a painting depicting the same outside scene with the tree. At first, it's not easy to detect. However, upon further study, the viewer sees that the image of the outdoor landscape is actually a duplication of the outdoor landscape, a replica image.

Magritte's art seems to ask us to understand that at first we only see what we want to see. Sometimes that desire to see life in a fixed way causes us to obscure reality. His paintings skillfully represent how easily we as humans paint fixed canvases in our

> SOMETIMES THAT DESIRE TO SEE LIFE IN A FIXED WAY CAUSES US TO OBSCURE REALITY.

minds. We create images reflecting our own personal belief systems of how we wish reality would be in order to avoid suffering. We don't like change. We like things to be predictable. Our negative thinking patterns are the same. We have a tendency to distort reality and perceive only what we desire to perceive. Like Magritte's *Human Condition* series, our fixed personal beliefs are temporarily relaxing and comforting to hold on to.

Perhaps we all prefer to live in the illusion of a universe that evokes allure and beauty instead of a world of fear. But we need the full picture, the reality of the good and the bad. To cultivate flexibility against the rigors of anxiety, Magritte's art can help us rewrite our outdated dictionary of personal beliefs that over the years come to feel as if they are etched in stone. If we acquire the knowledge to reduce excessive worry via reexamination, perhaps even through artistic effectiveness, we can do the same with our grief.

ANXIETY AS AN ASSET

In a similar way that we looked at depression as an undesirable catalyst to countless benefits like increasing the sensitivity of the heart, cultivating compassion for others, and fueling creativity, what if stress and anxiety could also be seen as assets? What if the much-maligned "worrisome nature" some of us have is an advantage instead of a burden? If our neurotic tendencies affect us so profoundly, could it be that over the millennia they have evolved for good reason? Apparently, the mental exercise of worry is compulsory to our human survival.

Worry comes with the unknown future. As mentioned earlier, it's beneficial for us to be wary of uncertainty. The lack of control of the future scares us for good reason. In a sense, human beings are prediction-making machines. Since primitive man, predicting the future as best we can is sometimes the difference between living and dying. Without worry, perhaps early humans would never have judiciously planned for future winters by finding shelter and stockpiling food. Or we would never have found ways to safeguard ourselves from rival tribes and ferocious animals. Anxiety about the future—with its possibilities and potential dangers—keeps our eyes focused on the prize of staying alive.

We don't pay enough attention to the bittersweetness of anxiety—that it is a complicated emotion. People who are fretful or neurotic are usually made fun of, but anxiety has qualities worth celebrating. Susan Cain, author of *Bittersweet*, said, "Neuroticism does have upsides. Despite their stressed immune systems, neurotics may live longer because they're vigilant types who take good care of their health. They're strivers, driven by fear of failure to succeed and by self-criticism to improve."[5] You don't have to be neurotic to experience this drive and desire to improve, but it *does* help to be keen-eyed to potential bumps on the road of life. It's not that we shouldn't worry; it's that we shouldn't panic.

In addition, many people with significant degrees of anxiety are focused and get things done on time. They are rarely

THE MAGIC IN THE TRAGIC

late and are extremely reliable. Why? Because they are too afraid *not* to be. Another advantage is that many sufferers are very effective in crisis situations and when placed in positions of responsibility. Because they're anxious anyway, a crisis or an emergency of some kind doesn't faze them. For some, it doesn't heighten the angst any more than it already has. In fact, focusing on someone or something else for a change helps distract them. It gets them out of their heads. Worry is their game, and under pressure, they can be tremendously helpful.

> FOR ANXIOUS PEOPLE, A CRISIS CAN LEVEL THE PLAYING FIELD AND REVEAL THE UPSIDE OF ANXIETY.

For anxious people, a crisis can level the playing field and reveal the upside of anxiety. A crisis gives anxious people permission to be scared for a legitimate reason. For a while, others can understand what it's like to feel on edge all the time. Chronic worry during non-crisis times can lead to shame if there isn't an identifiable stressor that a normal person can see. How many times have you heard people say, "Hey, just chill out!" Or, "Relax, there's nothing to be scared about. Stop worrying so much!" An emergency validates the psychic pain of the worrier so significantly that sufferers feel less pathologized.

In her eye-opening book *Andy Warhol Was a Hoarder*, Claudia Kalb drew attention to great minds that may have suffered from mental illness.[6] One of her most interesting analyses is of Charles Darwin. In addition to suffering from anxiety and a tormented need for order and perfection, he also sustained chronic physical illnesses. According to Kalb, he grappled with digestive dysfunction, muscle weakness, fatigue, headaches, dizziness, nausea, and vomiting. "He was a worrier. He fretted about his children, about his deadlines, about his reputation and always about what ailed him," said Kalb.[7] Besides hypochondria, his primary mental health issue, Darwin may have also suffered from agoraphobia, obsessive compulsive disorder, panic disorder, and social anxiety.[8] All these disorders can be incapacitating in today's world. Imagine suffering from these afflictions in the 1800s.

Given these probable mental conditions and his ill health, Darwin seems like the most unlikely naturalist to be visiting foreign lands gathering data for scientific research. Any person afflicted with extreme anxiety and gastrointestinal issues wouldn't likely embark on sea voyages for several months in dingy, primitive travel accommodations. Yet Darwin was still able to do all this, changing the world and the way we see it. Darwin wrote to a friend about his need to explore and travel: "I look forward even to seasickness with something like satisfaction, anything must be better than this state of anxiety."[9]

How did Darwin accomplish so much travel and research, a life's work of science and progress, with what could have been debilitating anxiety? Perhaps his anxiety and excessive worry gave him the boost he needed to complete his work. Maybe the stress of deadlines and his fear of defiling his reputation drove him to triumph. Is Darwin unique? Or a freak? Sounds like positive, vigorous neuroticism to me. For Darwin to succeed, he must have been able to put his organizing principles to good work and use his anxiety to help him.

THE MAGIC IN THE TRAGIC

CHALLENGING FIXED NEGATIVE THOUGHTS

An important part of cognitive behavioral therapy is identifying what you are specifically thinking when you are feeling anxious or distressed. Then, by naming these thoughts as cognitive distortions or organizing principles, you begin the process of externalizing them as something outside you, instead of an inherent part of you. If you literally relabel your fearful thoughts, worried thoughts, and even sad thoughts as cognitive distortions instead of believing them to be true, you can prevent them from adversely influencing your state of reality. This is a key step in building emotional resilience.

Here is an example of this process.

> **Fixed thought:** *Since my husband died, I am afraid to get close to anyone again. The feelings of abandonment are too painful. I can't go through another loss. I won't survive it.*
>
> **Flexible thought:** *My fears about getting close to people are completely understandable given what I've just lost. It's okay to feel scared to love someone again. This is just my fear trying to protect me. I have been through worse.*

Like my former patient Tyler, just because you have a distressing thought doesn't mean it's real. And if it's a futuristic worry, it doesn't necessarily mean the bad thing is going to happen. Remember René Magritte's paintings of the human condition: Don't take thoughts at face value. Give them a deeper examination. Ask: *Is this a real concern? Is reality being obscured by something—my first impression, previous experience, spiraling thoughts?* By stepping back and observing our thoughts objectively, we can change how we perceive negative thoughts and reduce their power over us. They lessen in strength because we see them for what they really are: uncomfortable thoughts that sometimes have no value whatsoever.

Here are some practical ways we can change our negative fixed thoughts.

1. Examine the Evidence

A good technique for challenging fixed beliefs and cognitive distortions is to separate yourself from emotional involvement with the negative thought. If you are confronted by an upsetting thought or an episode of irrational thinking, examine the evidence by looking deeply into the statements you are telling yourself. Ask: *Is this an opinion or absolute fact? Is it interpretation or reality?*

For example, statements such as "I am a loser" and "I will never succeed at anything in my life" are opinions. "Monday is my day to take the trash out to the curb" or "I forgot to feed the dogs" are facts. Segregating facts from opinions can help you determine which are likely to be a component of cognitive distortions instead of something based in reality. Otherwise, your thoughts become believable truths, predictions, or projections.

2. Stop with Double Standards

When we struggle with cognitive distortions about ourselves, we often use different standards for other people compared to us. For example, when we are self-critical, if we stop and think about the quality of that harshness, we know that we probably wouldn't speak to someone else that way. We are always much harder on ourselves than the people we care about in our lives, whether it's a friend or family member.

Instead of treating yourself with a different standard that you would never hold anyone else to, why not try using one standard for everyone, including yourself? Imagine telling a friend who had just started his own business, "It's going to fail just like everything else in your life." You would never say something like that to your friend, but you may to yourself. The next time you are beating yourself up about a mistake you made, ask yourself, *Would I speak to my friends this way?*

3. Be Aware of Absolute Language

When a person uses far-reaching, generalized statements that include words like *should, shouldn't, never,* and *always,* they're applying a set of unwritten rules to their thinking that can cause long-term anxiety. These are called "absolute statements," which, most of the time, are irrational or exaggerated versions of reality based on assumptions that humans (or the individual, at least) should act and feel a certain way. Most of the time, these irrational thoughts are untrue. For example, statements like "I will never be happy," or "I will always be a failure," or "I should be more productive at work," or "I should exercise more." (Notice the words *should, never,* and *always* used in each statement.) Some of these might have merit to them or come from a sound place, but when the individual puts strong conditions on these words, it sets a standard that is not humanly possible to achieve.

When you find yourself using a "should" statement, try substituting it with "I would prefer." For example, "I would have preferred to go to the gym this afternoon instead of going straight home." Does it lessen the impact for you? Does it free you from feeling inferior or guilty? "I would prefer" removes the person from being in a position of fault.

4. Examine Personal Labels

When we refer to ourselves with negative labels, like "inferior" or "a failure," that can also be a recipe for anxiety and distress. By examining these and other negative personal labels, we often see that they more closely represent specific behaviors or an identifiable pattern instead of the total person. For example, failing a test doesn't make the person a failure.

Once we start delving into what's behind a label and asking questions about the definitions we assign, the results can be surprising. For instance, what does it mean to think of yourself as inferior? Inferior to whom? Others at your workplace? Aren't they all inferior to someone else too? The more questions you ask when you challenge the definition of a label, the more you may come to realize how pointless such labels are, especially when applied to ourselves.

There's a good chance that based on a few experiences in

the past, you made up that negative label for yourself a long time ago (you made it an organizing principle). It's an adopted identity you've been carrying for years. But it may not fit who you really are today.

5. Employ Cost-Benefit Analysis

This method for challenging a negative thought relies on motivation rather than facts to help a person undo a cognitive distortion. In this technique, it is helpful to list the advantages and disadvantages of feelings, thoughts, and behaviors.

A cost-benefit analysis will help a person figure out what they are gaining by believing the negative thought and what they are gaining from always feeling bad about it. If you find the disadvantages of believing a thought outweigh the advantages, you'll find it easier to talk back and refute the irrational belief.

Ask yourself, *How does believing this negative thought help me build emotional resilience? How does feeling negatively about myself improve my life?* Your honest and genuine appraisal of these thoughts will help you be more accountable to yourself.

TRY THIS PRACTICE

Reducing Worry

When my patients are suffering from excessive worry to the point of feeling numb and detached from their true emotions, I often ask them to listen to particular pieces of music that will bring them back to themselves. The music I ask them to select is usually the soft, contemplative kind, to act as an inducer for self-reflection.

Over time, whenever they hear the song, it cues their mind to pause and relax. It signals their inner voice that it's time to turn down their senses. As they hear the music, they get centered. They connect with a different part of their soul, a part of them that is compassionate and emotionally linked to others. Suddenly they feel less alone. This exercise has a way of miraculously stopping the worry in its tracks. Why? Because it shifts the mind from *controlling* thinking to *insightful* thinking. The therapeutic benefit is that melancholic feelings, although they are often uncomfortable, ground us in reality.

During acute episodes of anxiety, where negative projections and fearful scenarios of the future are all-consuming, exposing oneself to sad music or to any art form that expresses human grief can decrease anxiety. Infusing the heart with meditative, sentimental music bursts that bubble.

The next time you find yourself worrying excessively about something and you feel your anxiety has escalated, try the following "inspiration exposure" exercise:

Step 1. Choose a favorite piece of sentimental music and begin listening to it. Pay attention to how the quality of the song pulls on your heartstrings. Do you relate to the lyrics, if there are any? Is it the melody that soothes you or reminds you of a happy time in your life? Or does it remind you of an unhappy time in your life that you survived?

Step 2. Write down five adjectives that describe what the song is evoking in your heart. For example: peaceful, calming, beautiful, tender, wistful, etc.

Step 3. Describe why you chose these adjectives. What part or aspect of the song is so peaceful, calming, beautiful? Be as specific as possible. This step could take up to five or ten minutes—the longer the better.

Step 4. Think of all the ways your life—past or present—possesses or once possessed the peaceful, calming, beautiful qualities you just identified. When did you experience these feelings? What activities and actions summoned them? What people in your life bring them out in you? What current or former activities align you with these feelings? Allow these questions to expand your introspection. As you follow the music, you may feel a curious transition from confusion to acceptance.

Asking these questions and connecting to the soulful part of you that is currently obscured by your worry is important. Remember, that soulful part of you is the *real you.* You are *not* just the nervous worrier that is trapped in a bubble of excessive fear. You are *not* all the scary uncertainties and obsessions you are spinning about. By getting your true "higher self" back, you will reduce your anxiety faster. The pivot from helpless worry to the grounded realization of who you *really* are makes the difference.

CHAPTER 7

THE MYTH OF CLOSURE

Slowing Down Our Timeline on Grief

No matter how bad your heart is broken,
the world doesn't stop for your grief.

FARAAZ KAZI

WHEN WE SUFFER A TRAGEDY, SUCH AS THE DEATH OF A LOVED one, or when we experience financial hardship, job loss, a divorce, or a breakup, eventually the word *closure* will float around. It floats like a mandatory step in a static protocol we are pressured to engage in. People seem to expect us to eventually "get over" the loss—to forget about it. This can be incredibly difficult with any kind of loss, but especially when it's the loss of a person. Human attachment does not easily dissolve. The bonds we developed with the loved one we've lost and the memories associated with them are immeasurable. Being told to get closure is like being asked to sever the ties we have with our newly departed ones—ties that can never really be severed.

The truth is, when someone close to us dies, looking for closure may be impossible, and it often feels inappropriate. It infers that we must somehow abruptly abandon our attachment or act like that person didn't matter as much as they did (or still do). Closure implies an ending. It implies we'll arrive at a single event or a destination where the grief stops.

For many, ideas of closure also suggest that to decrease suffering we must rapidly attain a state of healing. We're told to quickly pick ourselves up, let go of the past, and focus on the living. But the oversimplification of closure as a hurried means of healing when tragedy strikes can impair our ability to learn to live with suffering and could even increase our suffering.

> WE DON'T JUST "GET OVER" GRIEF; WE LEARN TO MAKE PEACE WITH ITS PRESENCE.

In contrast, taking time to process the grief and allowing ourselves room to mourn can decrease our suffering in the long run—and is as natural to life as breathing and laughing. It can be a long process with no timeline. It has no rules. It has no protocol. Author Marisa Renee Lee stated, "Grief is the repeated experience of learning to live in the midst of a significant loss."[1] We don't just "get over" grief; we learn to make peace with its presence.

THE MYTH OF CLOSURE

OUR CULTURE'S RESPONSE TO GRIEF

Our culture tends to avoid grief and all emotions that are considered negative. Instead, people place great emphasis on joy and happiness. We don't like suffering. We don't like to feel *any* pain. And, for many, extended grief is unbecoming—a sign of weakness. As a result, we're told to expedite the grief process with statements like, *Let it go! If you keep thinking about it, you'll never move on. Stop living in the past. The sooner you forget, the better you'll feel.*

Because grief is often misunderstood, the griever is often left to mourn alone. Ella Wheeler Wilcox's quote rings true: "Laugh and the world laughs with you, weep and you weep alone."[2] But did you know that crying and laughter have similar emotional benefits? First, they both reduce stress and are both considered natural painkillers.[3] Laughter releases serotonin and endorphins, which make us feel good. Crying releases oxytocin and, interestingly, releases inborn opioids that are biologically designed to numb pain. Hence, when it comes to tears, it's healthier to release them instead of suppressing them.[4]

Mourning is as essential to the human experience as all our emotions are. It's a part of life. Nothing more, nothing less. Yet grief in our culture is veiled in shame and clandestineness. It does not get the same attention that more jubilant emotions garner. For instance, we sometimes give ourselves permission to cry when justifiable tragedy strikes. But we are quick to hide our tears for seemingly lesser sorrows for

THE MAGIC IN THE TRAGIC

fear of ridicule. The irony here is that appropriately grieving any kind of loss is the elixir for healing. What we shun most as a society is what we need most. Our society today banishes grief. The ancient Greeks would be rolling in their graves.

COMFORT INSTEAD OF CLOSURE

In March 2014, CNN's Anderson Cooper was interviewing a psychologist in Kuala Lumpur, Malaysia, who was grief counseling families of the victims of the Malaysia Airlines flight MH370 that had vanished in the Indian Ocean.[5] Despite the fact that there was still no confirmation that lives had been lost—because the plane had still not been found—the worst was feared. As each day passed with no word on the whereabouts of the fated jet, hopes began to dash.

During the interview, when Mr. Cooper sensitively asked the psychologist the almost obligatory question—*How do you help people achieve closure after an event like this?*—the psychologist humbly prefaced his answer by saying that for him the word *closure* was the worst word to use after a tragic event of this magnitude. There was simply no such thing. He implied that the best he could offer them was the kind of human support that does not involve finding solutions or following any psychological protocol. All he could hope for was to comfort them.[6]

Rather than a path toward closure, bereavement or

THE MYTH OF CLOSURE

grieving is more about the mind, the heart, and the soul of the griever learning to coexist with deep wounds that never heal. Grief is a scar that leaves a mark and remains visible for life. Over time, the scar fades but never disappears entirely.

When both my parents died in 2004, the heaviness of my grief crashed into me like a freight train. More than twenty years later, I manage to comfort myself by filling my home with photos of my mother and father in happier times when they were healthy and unburdened by their illnesses. The sorrowful ache is still there, even now. Remembering them and the pain they went through is like running my fingers along the scar every day. Sometimes the nerve endings are so sensitive that it hurts to look back. But I do it because teaching my heart how to live with the sadness is more important.

GRIEF IS NOT ON A TIMELINE

After a loved one dies, we begin a personal journey of emotionally evolving and growing into a different kind of self-awareness. This new self-awareness helps us make the unspoken yet necessary agreement with ourselves to submit and live by life's terms, which means that over the course of our lives people we love will die. How we respond to it is up to us. No one is allowed to tell us when we are done grieving because it's not quantifiable and it's not linear.

The renowned Five Stages of Grief conceived by Swiss American psychiatrist Elisabeth Kübler-Ross allows for a very humanistic, nonlinear experience of grieving.[7] The stages are denial, anger, bargaining, depression, and acceptance. Although the theory sprang from her many years of working with the terminally ill, the emotional stages have been widely used to blueprint and track an individual's delicate process through any experience of loss. With regard to surviving a loved one's death, the griever will experience the stages in their own specific way and in no particular order. Kübler-Ross also emphasized that the stages she introduced are not intended to be a complete list of all possible emotions that could be felt. Her five stages are just a sampling.[8]

For Kübler-Ross, the stages of grieving were intended to help the sufferer work through each stage at their own pace. There is no timeline restriction. Sometimes individuals take three steps forward in their grieving and then the following week, two steps back. The resolution of each stage in a well-timed and systematic fashion is not required. The stages are merely pivotal points in time of the bereavement process that are experienced from a phenomenological standpoint, not a mandatory one.

It's important to remember that traversing through the grief and loss continuum at any level is a lifelong course. We don't try and accelerate it. The human heart is not a car engine that can be greased, oiled, and tuned up to perform better. It's not a bad idea to look under the hood every now and then, but you may not always find the answers in there. Gary

> TRAVERSING THROUGH THE GRIEF AND LOSS CONTINUUM AT ANY LEVEL IS A LIFELONG COURSE.

THE MYTH OF CLOSURE

Greenberg, author of *The Book of Woe: The DSM and the Unmasking of Psychiatry*, reminded us, "We can mourn the loss of anything to which we have become attached: a pet, a job, a home, a way of life. In bereavement, what is best about us—our ability to love—becomes the source of our suffering."[9] Consequently, if our capacity to become emotionally attached does not discriminate, neither does grief. No human heart is spared the true nature of its vulnerability.

So, we try to look at grieving as a beginning—albeit an involuntary one—to a new life of learning to dignify the suffering we are absorbed by. Like the concept of constructive aching, the new beginning asks the opposite of what closure expects of us. It asks us to learn to live with *not* forgetting and *not* getting over it—because we can't. We learn to coexist with the liability of owning a human heart and the constant reminder that we will always be scarred. But that scar has resilience-building qualities. It prepares the psyche for future inevitabilities that will come. Marcel Proust wrote, "Happiness is beneficial for the body but it is grief that develops the powers of the mind."[10] The treasured *magic in the tragic* perspective that we gain from referring to that scar periodically reminds us that we can handle this despite the horrible pain. In other words, we yield to the finite nature of all mortal relationships. We are born, we get attached, we love, and then, inevitably, we die.

> "HAPPINESS IS BENEFICIAL FOR THE BODY BUT IT IS GRIEF THAT DEVELOPS THE POWERS OF THE MIND."

THE MAGIC IN THE TRAGIC

GRIEF ON DISPLAY IN ART

The Romanian-born artist Albert György found meaning in his sorrow after the premature death of his first wife. In his isolation and extreme sadness, the artist presumably found a way to cope with his grief through sculpture. The bronze statue *Melancholy* (2012) was conceived as an expression of his raw heartbreak.[11] In creating the expressive statue, György perhaps chose *not* to forget his wife's death. He chose *not* to "get over it." He chose instead to coexist with tragedy instead of trying to "move on" from it.

Remarkably, the result of his pain has brought relief to millions of people who have viewed his sculpture where it sits in a park in Geneva. The well-known work depicts an abstract human figure sitting on a bench with its head and shoulders slumped over. A massive space of nothingness pervades the middle of its torso. The hollow center dominates the work by taking up most of the body. Its arms are crossed in an attempt to comfort the concavity in its chest. The rest of the physique is disproportionately slim and sticklike.

Maybe the giant hole represents the void that György felt after his loss. The abject barrenness is palpable. Conceivably the deep hole is an interpretation of how desolate he felt without the words to convey it. Or was he illustrating that a part of us can be brutally gouged away from our souls, resulting in a gaping abyss that can never be filled? The piece astoundingly acts as a distinguishing agent of human suffering. It's also a relatable work of art that has the connective power to bring people together in the common knowledge that we don't have to face these hardships alone. The statue *Melancoly* acts as a vehicle to help ease the self-consciousness of grieving openly.

Even viewers who find the distorted portrayal of the human frame displeasing to their artistic sensibilities are jarred by its evocative nature. You can't stop looking at it. It will make you feel something either way. To me, observing the sculpture is a mental reset. It helps me get reacquainted with the unspoken, poetic dialect of grief. It's a prevailing representation of how we can embrace beauty that is often spawned by grief. The statue even helps me fill my own emptiness by inducing a mindful instant of silence. It precipitates a brief "me-time" interval that sobers me to the reality of being human.

THE IMPORTANCE OF FUNERALS AND MEMORIALS

Human beings were meant to express their pain and grieve together despite how self-conscious it might make us feel. "There is no grief like the grief which does not speak," said Henry Wadsworth Longfellow.[12] So for hundreds, perhaps thousands of years, memorials and funerals for the departed have given survivors an opportunity to process death together and grieve in a healthy manner, instead of isolating from social interaction and preventing the human heart from naturally feeling the pain of loss.

THE MAGIC IN THE TRAGIC

Generations and centuries past, funeral processions marched through villages and cities, inspiring entire communities to pause together and show respect. Mourners congregated in town squares and places of worship to process and discuss the deaths of neighbors and friends. They gathered to share their sorrow so their pain could be witnessed. They gathered to show that the departed person's life mattered. It is still now as it was then: Survivors heal by showing up for and comforting one another.

On January 26, 2020, a few months before our nation went into COVID lockdown, former Los Angeles Laker and NBA superstar Kobe Bryant died in a tragic helicopter accident along with his daughter Gianna and seven other passengers. The fatal accident stunned the world and sent many Los Angelenos into shock over so many young lives taken so soon.

Within hours of his death, Bryant fans gathered outside the Staples Center Arena in downtown Los Angeles where Bryant won many championships for the Lakers. Each day, the number of mourners multiplied. Eventually it grew to hundreds, maybe thousands, of complete strangers milling about day and night sharing stories and memories about Kobe's greatness. They erected makeshift memorials of candles, photographs, flowers, signed basketballs, and Laker jerseys. The media could not stay away either; coverage of the mourners went on for weeks. It reminded me of the global response to Princess Diana's untimely death in 1997. Similar provisional memorials were erected all over the world, and the bereavement over her loss still lingers today.

THE MYTH OF CLOSURE

Both Princess Diana's and Kobe's deaths left a deep wound in the culture. And within that pain, fans and admirers all shared a desire to be together despite not even knowing one another. It comforted them. They could appreciate together their joy in watching Kobe play, and how fortunate they were to have been alive to witness his greatness. The common bond was in their shared sorrow. It's akin to the old proverb, "Shared joy is double joy; shared sorrow is half sorrow."

HONORING THE DEPARTED

If we don't mourn properly, it can stunt the grieving process. We can develop the kind of debilitating trauma that leads to long-term, complex grief. During the pandemic, many survivors of the victims of COVID-19 were prohibited from carrying out proper burials and memorials due to fear of infection. The survivors were unceremoniously deprived of a dignified burial for their loved ones.

Today, there isn't enough research out there yet to help us determine the psychological effects of that deprivation on the human mind.[13] The protracted bereavement minus the chance to release the pain and bury our loved ones could have devastating effects. In July 2021, *New York Times* writer Eduardo Medina wrote about a kind of "grief purgatory" that mourning families were stuck in: "Those who lost someone to Covid-19 are at an increased risk of developing prolonged grief disorder in which a person's bereavement is so intense that it disrupts day-to-day activities."[14] Without the ability to honor our departed loved ones, we are prevented from alleviating some of the torment of our grief.

> THE MORE DEVOTION WE GIVE TO THE DEAD, THE MORE WE EVOLVE AND GROW.

The more devotion we give to the dead, the more we evolve and grow. This is why funeral orations and eulogies are so important when people die. It provides an opportunity for release and to tell instructive stories we can learn from and explain why the departed meant so much to the community.

The ancient Greeks believed that paying respectful homage to the dead helps us understand what it takes to go on living. In 441 BC, Greek playwright Sophocles wrote *Antigone*, one of the greatest tragedies in the history of stage.[15] The intrepid heroine, Antigone, is faced with a grave decision after one of her brothers, Polyneices, is denied an honorable burial by Creon, the king of Thebes. Before the play starts, the brothers Eteocles and Polyneices, leading opposing sides in Thebes's civil war, die fighting each other for the throne. Creon decides that only Eteocles will be posthumously honored and Polyneices will be consigned to public shame. Polyneices' body would be denied holy rites and would be discarded and left unburied on the battlefield, which was the harshest, most discrediting punishment at the time. Antigone is outraged by this decree. But if Antigone disobeys her king and independently buries her brother with a proper funeral befitting a fallen warrior, she herself faces death.

In the end, Antigone remains true to both her heart and her brother. She defies her king because she believes in higher principles—her credence that natural law of human decency transcends the legal system. She moves forward and buries her disgraced brother. Even when faced with death, she refuses to go against either one. Creon sentences Antigone to death for her crime, and before he can change his mind she kills herself, dying a tragic hero. Antigone proudly defends her fatal decision: "I will bury him myself. And even if I die in the act, that death will be glory. I will lie with the one I love and loved by him—an outrage sacred to the gods."[16]

Sophocles understood the value and importance of speaking our grief and allowing the heart to find solace in proper mourning. "Strained silence, so I deem, is no less ominous than excessive grief," his Greek chorus declared.[17] He comprehended the enormous weight we carry when we deprive ourselves the ability to express our pain. He also related to the social ramifications of loyalty, integrity, and personal conviction. Antigone would be unable to live with herself without the curative, healing process of paying tribute to her brother's life and death.

For most of us, the death of a loved one requires recognition of the loss. It needs others to bear witness to not only our pain but to how much the departed's life meant to us. In some cases, it softens the blow of the death and makes it feel like they didn't die in vain. If Antigone lived, she might never have healed from her wounds, but her brother's burial was one way to venerate the loss and lionize his memory.

TRY THIS PRACTICE

Grief Exposure Exercise

Think of an event in your life that you still feel grief about but perhaps you have felt reluctant to share with others. For many this might be a difficult exercise, but in the long run, it will loosen the tight grip your pain has on you. Remember, it does not have to be the loss of a loved one. It can be the painful breakup of a relationship, a divorce, a financial loss, a job or business loss, a move, a missed opportunity, a decision you regret making, or even something you gave away.

Then break down the event into four parts: trigger, significance, interpretation, and replacement thought.

1. Trigger: A trigger is a reminder of the origin of your grief or an event that caused your pain to come back.

What is a trigger for your event?

Example:

- *A memory of an unexpected death of a family member.*

2. Significance: Significance is defining why this loss affected you so much.

Why was this person so important to you? Or why was this event (if not a person) so impactful? What are the specific feelings you have attached to this loss?

Examples:

- *I was very close to this family member.*
- *We talked on the phone every day.*
- *They gave me comfort and support during difficult times.*
- *They were my best friend.*
- *Every time I think about it, it makes me inconsolably sad.*

3. **Interpretation:** Interpretation is the meaning you attach to the event. In other words, it's the story you have created in your mind about the event that might be fueling the pain even more. It may include why it's better for you *not* to revisit the memory of the loss.

    How are you making sense of your loss?

    Examples:

    - *It's not fair; I never got to say goodbye.*
    - *I feel guilty because I never got to tell them I was sorry for bad arguments we had in the past.*
    - *I shouldn't have been so selfish.*
    - *If I think about it too much, I will spiral down into a deep depression.*
    - *If I think about it too much, I will never stop crying and I won't be able to function.*

4. **Replacement Thought:** The replacement thought is your opportunity to introduce the art of "inspiration exposure" and convert the perhaps negative interpretation into a *magic in the tragic* reaction

that will help you soften the sting of the loss. The alternative response is intended to transform your pain into constructive aching and to feel the grief as positive wounding.

What is a replacement thought for your event?

Examples:

- *In the spirit of bringing beauty to all my tragic experiences in life, today I will accept the discomfort of the loss (family member's death). I will not dwell on the fact that they are gone, but I will rejoice that they existed and I had the privilege of knowing them.*
- *For today, I'm going to honor my departed one by remembering the fun and happy times we enjoyed together. I will honor them by recalling the music we both liked, the places we liked visiting together, the TV shows and movies we laughed at, the kind of art we were both inspired by. I will recall all the meaningful conversations we had, the loving support we gave each other.*
- *Although their loss feels irreplaceable, I know that if I can feel that kind of connection with someone, I can find it again with others.*

This daily exercise with your unresolved grief from the past is effective only if it is performed consistently. Try to alter your responses each time you perform it. This will create more depth in your process. You will be amazed as you watch your stagnant sorrow transform into appreciation.

CHAPTER 8

MINDFULNESS

Developing an Alternative Relationship with Discomfort

Leave your front door and back door open.
Let thoughts come and go. Just don't serve them tea.

SHUNRYU SUZUKI

IN MY MIDTWENTIES, I WAS IN CRISIS OVER SEVERAL LIFE issues that were negatively affecting me. I was so fearful of my emotions that at times I could hardly sit still. Even in the cozy confines of my therapist's office, I would frequently pace back and forth, hoping to somehow ward off my psychic pain.

One day, my therapist, Claire, asked me what would happen if I allowed the emotional discomfort to just *be*. In other words, not fight it and instead imagine cultivating a new response to it. I soon realized that *nothing* bad would happen except feeling ill at ease for a while. Consequently, I began developing a different orientation around my emotional discomfort, one of acknowledgment instead of resistance. But without having been prompted to heighten my awareness to it, I might have continued believing that my pain was insufferable.

It's a fact: We all hate discomfort, especially the emotional kind. Many of us avoid thinking about our emotions and our pain at all costs. We'll take any mental distraction we can, change the conversation, repress the memory—if it means we can sidestep the hard and the heavy. But one therapeutic technique can actually help us tolerate our pain better by building a new affiliation with it. Sounds unlikely, right? A new relationship with pain? But it works. It's called mindfulness, and over the last decade, more people have been tapping into its calming powers than ever before.

Mindfulness, according to Jon Kabat-Zinn, is defined as a state of detached awareness of one's experience without judgment or reaction.[1] Mindfulness is when we turn on the "conscious awareness" switch and allow the mind to experience a negative stimulus—like a distressing thought or a feeling of unease—in a nonjudgmental way that places us in a spectator position. It's a way to identify and observe negative thoughts and feelings in the here and now by responding to them more reflectively instead of reactively.

There are many benefits to practicing mindfulness on the grief journey. It can help you:

- remain in contact with the present moment rather than engage in constant "fear-casting" about future catastrophic events;

- accept your life as it is right now, without the constant struggle and resistance;
- not assume your negative thoughts are facts, rather than just words happening in your mind;
- remember that what you are feeling is discomfort and *not* danger.

When we practice mindfulness during or after great loss, we are creating an alternate relationship with discomfort. We are learning to be okay with loss, even if it's the worst possible thing we could have imagined. Eckhart Tolle talked about how "accepting the unacceptable" is one of the most important strengths that any human being can develop.[2]

Because feelings of unease are such a big part of life, gentle exposure to that unease via mindfulness helps to slowly transform it into empowerment. For instance, whenever we suffer from what we think is "unacceptable" stress or anxiety, we tend to think in extremes. We catastrophize and think of worst-case scenarios. When we feel discomfort and develop a knee-jerk aversion to any uncertainty, we stray from conscious awareness and do everything in our power to attain a sense of safety, even if it's a false safety. We then emotionally dysregulate and all hell breaks loose. Emotional dysregulation is when we lose our ability to control emotions and how they affect us. It causes us to get further and further away from understanding ourselves.

We need mindfulness because we need to listen to what's going on in our inner world. One of the reasons I became a

THE MAGIC IN THE TRAGIC

WE NEED MINDFULNESS BECAUSE WE NEED TO LISTEN TO WHAT'S GOING ON IN OUR INNER WORLD.

psychotherapist—and it took me a long time to figure this out—is that when I was a boy, I was raised in a strict environment where children were not listened to. Children were expected to defer to the heads of the household and keep thoughts and feelings to themselves. Although I felt loved, I was not heard. My obedience was more important than my words or my feelings. Over time, I got stuck in believing that the only way I could belong in my family was to be seen and not heard, to never make mistakes and to always "do" the right thing. I became a human doing instead of a human being.

This was a problem for me. I was a sensitive, edgy kid who felt feelings deeply. Life's ups and downs got the best of me too easily. Now I can see how I would have benefited from the occasional opportunity to express my authentic thoughts and feelings to somebody, anybody, but I was prohibited from doing so. Years later, I decided that if being listened to was not in the cards for me, perhaps I could be a good listener to others. Maybe I could give to others what I was deprived of.

To this day, it still gives me joy to offer anyone unreserved attention and the time to just listen to them. Deep down we all want to be seen and heard. And along the way, I started listening to myself the way I was listening to my patients. I offered myself the same compassion I was giving them. Through mindfulness practice my conscious awareness grew, and listening to myself intently suddenly became a revelation to me.

THE ROLE OF MINDFULNESS PRACTICE

Mindfulness asks us to pause and step back when we get triggered and to learn to delay our automatic reactions. In his masterful self-help offering *Mindfulness in Plain English*, Buddhist monk and author Bhante Henepola Gunaratana said mindfulness is "observing the passing flow of experience. It is watching things as they are changing. . . . It is observing all phenomena—physical, mental, or emotional—whatever is presently taking place in the mind."[3] When we observe the "passing flow of experience" in our own lives—including loss and grief—we create an interval in between the moment we are activated and how we react to it. That interval, the ultimate moment of mindful "observation," even if it's just two to three seconds, is key to symptom management. It's where we acquire the ability to raise our distress tolerance thresholds and rewire our brains.

Clinical psychologist, author, and yoga teacher Dr. Bo Forbes said it this way: "You are an emotional electrician; you can learn to rewire yourself in healthier ways."[4] The human brain is capable of tremendous alteration with its neuroplasticity. We can actually get in there and do the work to become healthier and emotionally resilient. But the key is consistency and repetition. "The brain transforms when we repeatedly practice a skill such as playing the piano or hitting a baseball," said Forbes.[5] It's the same with our thoughts and feelings. When we consistently practice mindfulness, we actually rewire our brains and how we think about ourselves and our situations.

To be open to that space between what's happening and our reaction to it, we need to listen to ourselves more intently. Mindfulness practice helps replace the exhausting act of over-analyzing negative thoughts with the awareness that we are simply just *experiencing* negative thoughts. Because we often take our thoughts at face value, we don't realize that sometimes our thoughts may not have *any* value. We might start to believe our erroneous thoughts and see them as projections and predictions, not what they really are. That's where the interval becomes so significant.

For example, notice the difference between these two statements:

1. *I am a failure.*
2. *I just noticed that I had a thought about being a failure.*

See the difference? It's subtle but game-changing. The first one, *I am a failure*, sounds like a concrete statement believed as fact. It comes across as an absolute belief held uncritically and would cause any person emotional reactivity. The second, *I just noticed that I had a thought about being a failure*, is a more contemplative response coming from the observer position. The second one is adopting conscious awareness, which allows enough separation for the observer to see the thought about failure nonjudgmentally. Again, failure is an event (or, in this case, just a thought), and not a person. It's not personal. The observer can purposefully draw awareness to the negative thought and ultimately build a new relationship with it.

MAGRITTE'S PAINTINGS: A LESSON IN OBSERVATION

Artist René Magritte's *Treachery of Images* paintings from the 1920s challenge our automatic thought processes. As discussed in chapter 6, his works ask us to examine our immediate impressions about what we see and to question whether or not thoughts are facts. His most famous "word" painting (many of Magritte's artworks had words written in them) is a modest painting of a smoking pipe with a solid yellow background and the words "*Ceci n'est pas une pipe*" below it. This phrase is French for "This is not a pipe." The painting is perceptibly not an actual pipe, but rather an image of a pipe.

Magritte wanted to shake up conventional thought about everyday objects as a way to enlighten and increase awareness. What is real, and what is just a representation of a thing? What is objective, and what is subjective? If we are not looking at a pipe, but a representation of a pipe, we can separate belief from reality. We can observe with the objective mind what may be subjective.

The same is true with mindfulness. We can observe our negative thoughts as depictions of what we are feeling, not necessarily reality. We may think we are inferior to others, but perhaps that's just an interpretation of ourselves. Just

THE MAGIC IN THE TRAGIC

> WE CAN OBSERVE OUR NEGATIVE THOUGHTS AS DEPICTIONS OF WHAT WE ARE FEELING, NOT NECESSARILY REALITY.

because we think something, that does not mean it's true, no matter how believable it appears. Magritte's painting also highlights the gap between thinking about something and then creating conscious meaning of it. When we recognize that gap, we can pause and expand our awareness of our reality. Otherwise, we will start seeing a real pipe in what is, in fact, a painting of a pipe.

The next time you're really stressed out about something and you're about to react to it negatively, consider the impartial watchfulness suggested by Gunaratana and remember Magritte's pipe painting. If you pause and wait a moment, you will see that your distressing thoughts and maybe even your feelings will slightly change. If you wait longer, you'll experience even more change. And so on. By doing this, you'll practice delaying instantaneous interpretations and will become a better listener, reflector, and observer to yourself.

FINDING YOUR QUIET MIND

Catastrophic events can make us realize how attached we are to the familiar. In his spiritual guidebook, *The Seven Spiritual Laws of Success*, Deepak Chopra taught us that "the search for security and certainty is actually an *attachment* to the known. And what is the known? The known is our past."[6] When our life is interrupted and the "known" is compromised, we stress.

But with mindfulness, we can create a new comfort zone. Not a comfort zone based on guarantees or immediate results. Not based on surface thinking or on future-based projections. And not based on the familiar and known. Rather, we can create a new comfort zone based on the present. Right now. This minute. And we do this by finding the *quiet mind*. The quiet mind is a state of consciousness where your mind is relaxed and your thoughts are not running rampant.

Imagine a vast ocean during a severe storm. Hurricane-like winds are blowing. Gigantic waves are crashing around. The ocean surface rises and falls with fierce unpredictability. Yet, regardless of the condition of the surface of the water, if we dip below and go underneath the surface, it is calm and peaceful. When we are stressed, our surface thoughts are the same: tumultuous, scary, erratic. We naturally feel uneasy. But when we practice taking a pause, it's like slipping underneath the ocean of your frightened, stormy thoughts and accessing the quiet of your mind.

Finding the quiet mind is not about avoiding uncertainty and fear but about how we relate to discomfort. In Chödrön's *Comfortable with Uncertainty: 108 Teachings on Cultivating Fearlessness and Compassion*, she demonstrated, via an ancient allegory from the Buddhist faith, how it is possible to pause in the very midst of distress. She wrote of a woman who finds herself on a cliffside with tigers above her and tigers below. In what could be a moment of panic, the woman sees a bunch of strawberries and pauses to eat them and enjoy them. She has not forgotten about her predicament. She may very well be at death's door. Yet she remains present and pauses to eat the strawberries. She savors the moment and makes it a precious one.[7]

The tigers in our lives will never stop coming. We will always experience some kind of human dilemma of varying degrees. But it behooves us to find these healthy intervals and recognize that the tigers chasing us might simply be our negative thoughts and our fearful projections. The *magic in the tragic* prompts us to transform our weakest, most helpless moments into precious ones. In other words, the strawberries we choose to eat may never taste as sweet without our life challenges. We can learn to take the precious pause, eat more strawberries—as the woman in the parable does—and reorient ourselves each time we feel panicked. This way we can alter our reality.

> THE MAGIC IN THE TRAGIC PROMPTS US TO TRANSFORM OUR WEAKEST, MOST HELPLESS MOMENTS INTO PRECIOUS ONES.

THE DECEPTION OF CONTROL

As we practice mindfulness and get more comfortable with the discomfort, we can let go of the need to have everything under control. In my therapy practice, instead of using the common deescalating statement, "Relax, everything is under control," I have my patients say, "Relax, nothing is under control." My patients don't always like this alteration, but I find it helpful.

If you acknowledge "*nothing* is under control," this liberating statement can help build emotional resilience. Believing you can control things, such as other people, traffic, the weather, the stock market, or anything else, is a frustrating, anxiety-producing, and futile investment of time and energy.

In contrast, surrendering to the acceptance that we have little or no control over things sets us up for success and productivity. It allows for the passing flow of experience where we do not immediately react to results and outcomes, but we observe the process in the precious pause. We don't have to perseverate and ruminate 24-7. Recognizing that you *don't* have control allows you to let go. It takes the responsibility and the burden of needing to carry the world off your shoulders. Letting go gives you peace of mind.

TRY THIS PRACTICE

Mindful Repetition

Here's a way to adopt new perspectives and add mindful insights to your daily living. As a psychotherapist, I have learned that repetition and reinforcement help a great deal during the process of building emotional resilience. Mindful reinforcement induces awareness, which opens up new possibilities of thinking and feeling.

I often ask my patients to think of a special word or phrase that holds meaning for them. I then ask them to write that special word or phrase on colored sticky notes and place them in strategic places in their homes or workplaces as reminders to pause and invite positive awareness to their day.

The sticky notes can be placed on your bathroom mirror—so they are the first things you see in the morning—or they could be placed on your refrigerator door, on the dashboard of your car, or any place that will force you to see them regularly.

Now, what do you write on the notes? Anything that feels positive. For example, two of my favorite words are *for now*. They indicate a temporary state, a helpful cue about the beauty of impermanence. So when I am feeling low, reminding myself that it's just *for now* is an advantageous prompt and helps me stay in that sweet spot of living with the transitory states of happiness and sadness.

Use any word or phrase that feels encouraging. Your word or words of affirmation can be anything you choose. They just need to have meaning and intention for you.

Here are some other examples:

- *Trying new things is healthy*
- *It's okay to change*
- *Let go*
- *There is no danger in letting go*
- *Quiet mind*
- *Be mindful*
- *Be an observer*
- *Be a spectator*
- *Be kind to yourself*
- *Be patient*
- *Slow down*
- *Self-compassion*
- *For now*
- *Focus*
- *This is not a pipe*
- *Tigers above, tigers below*

If you can begin by completing this exercise every morning for just one week, you are already inviting mindfulness into your life. Big things have small beginnings.

CHAPTER 9

THE POWER OF SELF-REGULATION

Deactivating the Threat Response

Sometimes the most important thing in a whole day is the rest we take between two deep breaths.

ETTY HILLESUM

TODAY, THE PRODIGIOUS DEMAND FOR MENTAL HEALTH services—due to loss, hardship, an unstable world, societal disruptions, and a decline in mental illness stigma—has skyrocketed to new heights. More people are seeking therapy than ever before. Consequently, the mental health treatment industry has grown exponentially. There is no shortage of therapeutic modalities, virtual or in-person, for every type of psychological condition from anxiety disorders to drug and alcohol addiction, to major depression, to severe trauma, and many other conditions. Yet science and research have recently discovered that many of these modalities and interventions are not always effective without a self-regulation component that addresses the body's built-in survival mechanism called the *threat response*.[1]

The threat response is the brain's first responder to any perceived danger. It's activated by the amygdala, the brain's fear center, which acts like an inner smoke detector that dispatches the fight-flight-freeze defense mechanism to go to work. The threat response mechanism is fail-safe—once it's triggered, the life-saving system is designed to immediately protect the organism no matter what, at all costs. It does not take a time out to scrutinize the danger or analyze whether the threat is real or imagined. Evolution has adapted it to act quickly—and for good reason. Our primitive ancestors faced immediate threats—animal predators, rival tribes, harsh elements, and other threats that would require an immediate survival plan. We may not face these same primitive threats regularly, but it's the same reaction in us that springs to action and impels us to find safety. The amygdala's stimulation of the threat response has been crucial over the millennia in giving us tools to defend ourselves and in perpetuating the existence of all living things. Even insects and plants have a similar defensive construct intended for self-preservation.

Not only do our threat responses activate our physical bodies for survival—our minds and emotions immediately engage too. Once activated, rational thought goes offline and our brains can go to extremes to manage the threat—we can think catastrophically, emotionally dysregulate, and become overwhelmed with unsettling anxiety symptoms. In other words, once the logical, "executive" brain becomes eclipsed by the "emotional" brain, panic can escalate and a war begins inside our minds. The rational mind fights for position against the instinctual, frightened mind. And when we are triggered, the emotional mind usually wins. This can result in distressing symptoms that can be debilitating, and if left untreated, can worsen into a chronic condition. A system that evolved to protect us has done its job so well it can actually harm us too. Overadaptation to our fear responses can make us so hypervigilant that we suffer.

SOMATIC THERAPY TO MANAGE ANXIETY

The human organism is a complex blend of mind, body, and emotion, which work in concert with one another. For too long many therapy practices have only sought to address thoughts and feelings. We are learning that one of the most critical pieces to helping people reduce distressing symptoms is by also addressing the body. In order to do so, we must learn the fundamental skill of self-modulating the central nervous system, which involves physiological activation. We must consider our physical selves in our healing process and as we endeavor to build emotional resiliency.

Cognitive behavioral therapy (CBT), a vital therapeutic approach to treating anxiety and many forms of trauma, works effectively to alter the mind's negative thinking patterns with thought restructuring. It rests on the premise that our perceptions are the major determinants of how we feel and act, and it asks the patient to focus on how those perceptions dictate reality. CBT suggests we examine our personal beliefs about ourselves, other people, the world, and what we hold to be true, and then targets faulty or irrational negative thinking patterns that may be distorting reality and causing distress. But it does not focus on the body. It bypasses the threat response and only addresses our thinking process.

All forms of emotional trauma get encoded in the senses, not just in conscious memory, and our central nervous system can remain fixed in threat response mode all the time, often unbeknownst to us. Because of this, the trauma stored in the body often does not get treated. As a result, symptoms of distress persist and the emotional dysregulation cycle remains intact. A type of therapeutic intervention that includes the body in its practice and helps to deactivate the threat response is called *somatic therapy* (or somatic resourcing).

Somatic therapy is a modality that focuses on how painful experiences are expressed and manifested in the body. The primary aim of somatic therapy—also known as "body psychotherapy"—is to reduce emotional discomfort by using mind-body techniques to release chronic tension and promote better mental health. Human beings store historical

THE POWER OF SELF-REGULATION

memories of grief, loss, pain, and many other emotional experiences on a cellular level. A 2017 study found that when we are chronically exposed to perceived danger, the structural, cellular mechanisms that govern stress resiliency and susceptibility are profoundly affected.[2] For example, when the human organism is threatened, trauma can be inscribed in the senses through hormonal messenger molecules. The molecules record the sensory impressions of the perceived threat as memory. This memory can later prompt the same knee-jerk response that was introduced by the original threat. It turns out it's not just "all in our heads," but our bodies hold the memories as well, according to Dr. Bessel van der Kolk, author of *The Body Keeps the Score*.[3]

Somatic therapy was originally created to help trauma survivors ultimately experience relief from their trauma symptoms such as flashbacks, insomnia, nightmares, and tumultuous relationships. But in the last several years, somatic therapy has become a widely used modality in helping individuals who struggle with all kinds of stressors.

> HUMAN BEINGS STORE HISTORICAL MEMORIES OF GRIEF, LOSS, PAIN, AND MANY OTHER EMOTIONAL EXPERIENCES ON A CELLULAR LEVEL.

SELF-REGULATION TO THE RESCUE

Therapy, and somatic therapy in particular, can help us manage our overactive and sometimes harmful threat responses on the clinical level. But what if therapy is not available to us? How do we manage our crippling anxiety in the day-to-day scenarios when our emotions go out of control? We self-regulate.

Self-regulation is the ability to manage disruptive emotions and impulses and be able to soothe and calm the body's reaction to stress. Self-regulation is the ability to interrupt the often-paralyzing threat response when it's happening, while you're fully engaged in the activities of daily living. This can be incredibly important in the grief process when it feels like your life is falling apart, you're prone to emotional irregularities, and the uncertainty of the future looms like a menacing threat. Knowing you have the capability to manage your overwhelming emotions is key to building emotional resilience.

Self-regulation techniques, such as mindfulness skills, diaphragmatic breathing, tension and release, and progressive muscle relaxation (all of which we'll explore later), help stimulate the natural stabilizer called the parasympathetic nervous system. This system is the primal mechanism we all possess that restores the body back to normal after the threat response is activated. Practicing self-regulation techniques relaxes the body by rebooting the prefrontal cortex (executive brain). The prefrontal cortex is involved in higher order brain functions such as sensory perception, cognition, planning, reasoning, and language. If we keep the executive brain online, we inhibit the threat response and activate the parasympathetic nervous system.

THE POWER OF SELF-REGULATION

THE SOOTHING MAGIC OF CLASSICAL MUSIC

One of the best ways to regulate emotions and overwhelming anxiety—which I personally attest to, and which I recommend to all my patients—is by listening to classical music. I discovered the powerful effects of classical music while grieving significant loss. Classical music activates positive effects in the brain, like empathy, intelligence, and confidence.[4] It also improves sleep patterns, reduces stress, lowers blood pressure, and helps with memory.[5] Exposure to a calming piece of classical music releases dopamine, which is the brain's organic "happy" chemical.[6] If we pay close attention to the music and allow it to engulf us in its comforting sound, it acts like a temporary central nervous system sedative and threat response deactivator.

An excellent self-regulation assistant and resilience builder is the adagio from Ludwig van Beethoven's Concerto No. 5 (*Emperor*), composed in 1809. Like many great artists and achievers featured in this book, Beethoven's deep understanding of human emotion may also have sprung from the ravages of tragedy, loss, and even abuse. In the book *Why Beethoven: A Phenomenon in One Hundred Pieces*, author Norman Lebrecht's case study on Beethoven reveals how he could never fully escape his dysfunctional childhood.[7] He was psychologically injured by his father's addiction to alcohol and punitive musical training. As a result, Beethoven never married. He avoided emotional attachment, feared stability, and avoided crowds. Yet Beethoven was a passionate

THE MAGIC IN THE TRAGIC

and tempestuous romantic who was as deeply affected by beauty as he was tormented by the women he could never get close to.

Fortunately for us, he had the uncanny ability to convert his adversity into his music. Beethoven historians tell us this work was his final concerto due to his complete loss of hearing.[8] How he was able to compose this piece, and many other masterpieces, without hearing is perhaps a testament to how aesthetically affecting the vibration of the music is. Perhaps the tonality of it is filled with such cosmic enchantment that it affects the soul on levels of awareness unknown to us yet.

> EVEN IF YOU'RE NOT A CLASSICAL MUSIC LOVER, YOU CAN'T HELP BUT BE EMOTIONALLY INFLUENCED BY ITS RAW AND SIMPLE REFINEMENT.

The delicate adagio (not the rondo or allegro) of *Emperor* has spiritual magic in its soothing yet melancholic tones. When we listen to this piece, a gentle stream of tranquility floods our consciousness. It is a mindfulness intervention I offer to my patients because it never fails to deliver. The gentle opening bars of the concerto anchor the mind and prompt wistful introspection. It's like a switch goes off in our heads and we slow down, we connect to our own self-effacement, and we temporarily let go of all the trivial things we are negatively perseverating about. The piece is extraordinarily moving, conveying frailty and poise in the same breath. Even if you're not a classical music lover, you can't help but be emotionally influenced by its raw and simple refinement.

Nearly a hundred years later, French post-impressionist

composer Maurice Ravel created the soft melody of *Pavane for a Dead Princess*, which offers similar emotional self-regulating effects. Written in 1899, the piece is a serene meditation of both sorrow and joy. Ravel, a friend of Clause Debussy, prided himself on simplicity and the opaqueness of his musical structure. Consequently, his works like *Pavane* summon our subjective, hidden emotions and unacknowledged feelings. Like Beethoven's concerto, it also prompts introspection and allows the mind to safely transcend discomfort through the inspiring sensation of its beautiful sound. Listening to *Pavane* is a therapeutic experience to say the least, because if you concentrate on what it evokes in you, time can stand still, and you might find yourself face-to-face with the purest form of here-and-now consciousness. An ideal adjunct for helping you deactivate the threat response.

Both Beethoven's concerto and Ravel's *Pavane* are unique kinds of musical pieces that can uplift us while simultaneously grounding us. For me, I've found other moving classical music pieces that have similar uplifting qualities are:

Gustave Mahler: Symphony No. 5, Adagietto
Jules Massenet: *Thaïs, Act II, Méditation* (arr. for piano and cello)
Edvard Grieg: Piano Concerto in A Minor, op. 16, Adagio
Camille Saint-Saens: *Le Cygne*
Robert Schumann: *Kinderszenen*, op. 15, *Träumerie* (arr. for cello and orchestra)

TRY THIS PRACTICE

Three-Minute Pause

The following is an outline of a practical, behavioral threat response intervention using the self-regulation techniques discussed earlier. The series of exercises should take only a few minutes total. I recommend trying it several times per day.

You can try this three-minute pause in a formal or informal setting—seated and focused, or during your normal activities.

- *Diaphragmatic Breathing (4–7–8 Method)*
- *Grounding*
- *Tension and Release*
- *Affirmations*
- *Music (optional)*

Formal Pause: Sit in a quiet place, or lie on your bed or on a yoga mat on the floor. It's best to close your eyes for this exercise. If you choose to sit, your posture should be dignified, yet relaxed. This exercise helps you to turn down your senses.

Informal Pause: You can do this anywhere—sitting at your desk at work or home, in your car (not while car is in motion), waiting at a doctor's office, taking a shower or bath, or any place or situation where you can safely pause from whatever you are doing and ground yourself for three minutes. When these short pockets of time present themselves, fill them with the following mindfulness exercise. It will help you create separation from your worries.

The pause exercise is designed for you to practice pulling back from a stressful moment and engaging your executive brain. When you are triggered, if you wait one minute, you will see that your distressing thoughts and maybe even your feelings will slightly change. If you wait two minutes, you'll experience even more change. If you wait three minutes, even more, and so on. Remember, accessing your executive brain also means you are checking in with your "higher" self—the part of you that is rational and balanced.

Many people make the mistake of only doing one mindfulness check-in per day. Some do lengthy meditations in the morning or perhaps a meditation in the evening. But, in my experience, when we check in for shorter periods of time several times a day (at least three times per day), it's much more effective in calming the central nervous system. The constant reinforcement (three minutes at a time) has longer-lasting effects. Because we are so easily derailed by the worries of life, our minds are incessantly working overtime. Hence, we need to hit the reset button throughout the day. Each time we reset and take a significant pause, we bring the rational mind back and we deactivate the threat response.

Diaphragmatic Breathing (4–7–8 Method)

Be mindfully aware that you are breathing by focusing on the inhale and exhale. Take a deep breath in that lasts for four seconds. Hold the breath for seven seconds. Then exhale through your nose for eight seconds. (I usually extend my exhale to ten or twelve seconds but whatever feels comfortable to you is best.)

While you are focusing on your breathing, try to become aware of yourself as an observer. Not your ego-self, not your conceptual-self, and not your projections about the future—your analytic thinking is an impediment here. This is a practice to get you in touch with your deeper self. As soon as your mind wanders to things you have to do today or to things you are worried about (and your mind will definitely wander), simply come back to the task of counting from the 4–7–8 breathing protocol. When your mind wanders again . . . you notice it, then you come back. Your mind wanders again . . . you notice it, then you come back. That back-and-forth activity is highly beneficial in building strong distress tolerance skills. Like a muscle, it needs to be exercised.

Grounding

As you focus on your breathing you will add a new layer of awareness. Ground yourself with sensory perception. Pay attention to the sounds you hear. Do you hear street noises? Do you hear the wind blowing against trees? Do you hear birds chirping? Do you hear cars driving by? Do you hear music? Also, can you smell anything? Freshly cut grass? Someone's home cooking? Car exhaust from the street?

Then, pay attention to what your body feels at

that moment. Is it tense? Is it relaxed? Does your body ache anywhere? Think of the points of contact where your body touches the chair, couch, or yoga mat you are sitting or lying on. Can you soften into it? Can you feel your back resting against it or your bottom sitting on it? Can you feel the floor under your feet? Be an observer and simply notice.

Tension and Release

The last layer of awareness is your muscles. Since you want to keep it short and simple, choose three to four parts of the body you want to focus on. For example, take your two hands and lightly squeeze them into a fist. Hold on to the soft tension for five to seven seconds. Then gently release the tension. Notice the new feeling of relaxation spreading from your wrists down to your fingertips.

Pick another set of muscles in your body and repeat the same exercise. For instance, gently tense your shoulders by scrunching or shrugging them up toward your head. Hold on to the soft tension for five to seven seconds. Then gently release the tension in your shoulders. Notice the new feeling of relaxation spreading from your arms to your shoulders.

Next, pull your feet back toward you. Hold on to the soft tension for five to seven seconds. Gently release the tension. Then, curl your toes forward, hold for five to seven seconds, then release. Notice the new feeling of relaxation spreading from your knees down to your feet.

While sitting in a chair, stretch your hip muscles by gently twisting your upper torso, but keep your lower body stationary. Repeat the same as above by noticing the soft tension for five to seven seconds, then noticing the relaxing release. Do both sides.

If you wish, you can continue to move through all the muscle groups in your body. This will naturally put your entire body at ease.

Although you were not aware, while you were in the process of squeezing and releasing, you were probably not thinking about your worries at all. You were instead focused on the physical sensations you were creating with your hands, shoulders, and feet.

Affirmations

The final component of the exercise is reciting affirmations while you are engaged in your pause. For example, as you are noticing your breathing or in the midst of grounding or in the tension and release mode, you can say or whisper to yourself:

- *For the next three minutes, it's okay for me to let go of my excessive need for control. Nothing is wrong.*
- *For the next three minutes, it's okay to allow myself to be imperfect. I am a human being, not a human doing.*
- *For the next three minutes, it's okay for me to feel uncomfortable about uncertainty. This is discomfort, not danger.*

- *For the next three minutes, it's okay for me to initiate self-care and be kind to myself. I deserve a break too.*

The pause is designed for you to practice mindfully noticing and observing your experience with your breathing, grounding, and tension and release. Eventually, your negative thoughts will also become things you are just "noticing" instead of disturbing interruptions that ruin your day.

The next time you are feeling stressed or you're in an extreme state of panic about anything, take the three minutes, pull back, and self-regulate. If you repeat this entire protocol at least three times per day, whether you are anxious or not, you will be majorly contributing to deactivating your threat response and calming your central nervous system. It will also help you begin the process of getting underneath your worries by changing your *response* to your worries.

In addition, this three-minute precious-pause exercise will teach you to slow down your life and commune with your higher self. The pause will inspire compassion for yourself each moment you stop, reset, and repeat the steps. It will bring you closer to respecting your psychic pain gracefully. Don't forget that your worry or panic is related to your temporary attachment to the familiar of desperately wanting quick answers—the kinds of answers that don't exist in the moment. Seeking instant relief will cause you more suffering.

Instead, commit to the long game. Nothing of value, even in the world of self-help and wellness, comes easily and swiftly. We all know how difficult it is for us to change and adopt new routines and rituals in our lives. We change by engaging in small, incremental alterations and shifts in behavior, sustained over time. So instead of searching for speedy and potentially unhealthy remedies to relieving your distress, stop and reset. If you practice this daily, you will be shocked at how much better you will start to feel. And, if the spirit moves you, especially in the morning, turn on the adagio from Beethoven's Concerto No. 5 or Ravel's *Pavane* as a companion to your pause.

CHAPTER 10

THE NEED FOR NOSTALGIA

Looking Back to Create a More Hopeful Future

*Life must be understood backwards,
but . . . it must be lived forwards.*

SØREN KIERKEGAARD

HAVE YOU EVER BEEN TEASED FOR BEING OVERLY NOSTALGIC? Or been embarrassed for talking about the way things used to be? For many people, being nostalgic means you're too sentimental. You're stuck in the past and are too scared to change. Or you're running from some menacing truth or from disturbing facts in your present life that you are too afraid to face, so you'd rather stick with a past you feel safer in. Especially after a great loss, you might even hear that you should stop looking back at a past that is long gone, and instead focus on the future.

In early 2003 I treated a fifty-eight-year-old dermatologist named Lydia for symptoms of depression, post-traumatic stress disorder, and insomnia. After tragically losing one of her adult daughters in the 9/11 attacks, her grief immobilized her. Returning to her normal activities of daily living seemed untenable. Her heart felt irrevocably shattered. As a result, she withdrew from family and friends and took a leave of absence from her medical practice.

She came to therapy not only because she needed help to work through her prolonged bereavement, but also because her family was concerned that her manner of grieving was becoming "obsessive."

Lydia reported that for the previous year she had ruminated about the tragedy on a daily basis. She spent inordinate amounts of time listening to her departed daughter Ava's favorite songs and compulsively watching old family videos until the wee hours of the night. Although the videos and the music gave her a sense of comfort, her husband and two living daughters worried about her constant need to dwell in the past.

Eventually, I invited the family to come in for a few sessions with Lydia. They slowly began to understand that Lydia was simply healing in her own way. The reliving of happy times with Ava helped her mourn the loss. Once the family was able to grasp the reality of the situation, it relieved their anxiety, and they could step back and be more patient with her.

THE NEED FOR NOSTALGIA

For Lydia, by respecting the need to reminisce, she unknowingly transformed her pain into grateful recognition. Her inner dialogue switched from dark absolutes like, *I will never see my daughter again* or *I will not survive this pain* to more assuaging thoughts like, *I'm happy to have known her* and *I will always remember her as a wonderful daughter who brought joy to everyone.*

> THE NEED TO REMINISCE CAN TRANSFORM PAIN INTO GRATEFUL RECOGNITION.

But without having indulged her suffering with healthy nostalgia, she might have remained stuck in the mire of her depressive symptoms. She might have missed out on the milestone of converting sorrow into *constructive aching* and *positive wounding.*

Even though some people discourage being nostalgic, as Lydia discovered, there are astonishing benefits to looking back and evoking the past. Nostalgia, or reminiscing, can be an effective facilitator for many positive things.

1. Nostalgia can cultivate gratitude.

For example, for someone grieving after the pandemic, temporarily reflecting on pre-pandemic times can be an effective means of finding gratitude and can help us look forward to the future by reconnecting us with the routines, habits, and rituals that have worked well for us in the past. Nostalgia assists us in remembering things we took for granted, like human touch, the company of others, social gatherings, access to museums, theaters, concerts, even travel. Or, if you've lost a loved one, looking back at the past can inspire deep appreciation for the meaningful and positive times you had with that person.

2. Nostalgia can help us prepare for the future.
By remembering the past and how good it was before, we are wisely fortifying ourselves for future catastrophes. Recalling "happy" times and identifying the conditions that promoted that happiness is valuable data for how to recreate that moving forward. Calling to mind the past could save your life.

3. Nostalgia naturally keeps us thinking positively.
If we can value the "looking back" at our past now, it could inspire hopefulness instead of despair. For example, remembering that we are capable of experiencing joy, of feeling free and hopeful again, is more important as we build emotional resilience. There is a big difference between wallowing in nostalgia and positively accessing it for good mental health purposes.

THE POWER OF DAYDREAMING

Just like being too nostalgic, the common act of daydreaming about the future gets a bad rap too. In our society, when you're daydreaming, this suggests you're not being productive and you're wasting precious time. Some people may think you're not serious or reliable because of this tendency.

But the field of neuroscience actually encourages

THE NEED FOR NOSTALGIA

daydreaming. Not the over-idealistic, impractical kind of fantasizing that is borderline delusion. But research shows that tiny respites that allow your mind to wander freely increase mental acuity by giving the mind a needed break.[1] It turns out that "zoning out" every now and then is good for you. It can also stimulate ambition, strengthen your self-esteem, elevate your mood, increase creativity, and help you focus better. Daydreaming can also assist in problem-solving, risk analysis, organizing, planning, and preparation. But most importantly, daydreaming is healthy because it helps us ward off despair. Imagining a better life for ourselves and our families and wishing for positive outcomes and happier times during any crisis we are experiencing keeps us going. Essentially, daydreaming inspires hopefulness.

In the 1947 film *The Secret Life of Walter Mitty*, the title character, played by Danny Kaye, is a clumsy, mild-mannered man who lives two lives—a surface life as a proofreader for a publishing company and an imaginary dream life of unlikely heroics. (A remake of the film starring Ben Stiller was released in 2013.) In the Danny Kaye version, Mitty has a penchant for escaping his henpecking, demanding mother and his mundane existence by mentally transporting himself to a fantasy life of adventure. He's an idealistic, scatterbrained individual who chronically detaches from reality through his daydreams and his whims. But what makes the absent-minded Walter Mitty so charismatic are the wildly vivid contexts of his fancies. In contrast to his bumbling personality, in each of his fancies, Mitty is instead sophisticated, talented, confident, and courageous—the direct opposite of who he is in his surface life. Some of his gallant daydreams include being a brilliant surgeon who saves lives and performs medical miracles, being an RAF Air Force pilot who shoots down Nazi planes in World War II, and being a brave sea captain who commandeers a ship during a raging storm. He even has fantasies where he is a singer and performer.

The hapless Mitty dwells so profoundly in his double life that his social functioning in his real life is inept at best. One might say that due to his caprices, he deprives himself of an authentic, real life. But does he really? In many ways I see Mitty's escapism as a coping skill that converts his meek perception of himself into something he can be proud of—perhaps a "higher self." The daily liaisons with his secret world give him something to aspire to, even if they seem overly idealistic. They light the fires of his dormant ambitions, and he comes alive.

Mitty's diversions pay off in the end. They prepare him for his real-life future because at the conclusion of the film, his musings of being a better version of himself help him change. After he accidentally gets involved in a true-life conflict of murder and espionage, the crisis induces him to step up and take on the more favorable version of himself. He solves the crime, the bad guys are apprehended, and he saves the day.

We can take a cue from Walter's example by engaging in flights of fancy when we are struggling—especially after a loss or change, when the future is uncertain. These are excellent times to dream a better future into reality.

HABITS TO HELP US PREDICT OUTCOMES

Another important tool for building emotional resilience is keeping our rituals, routines, and habits intact despite what's going on around us. Without the consistency of these central, everyday behaviors, our lives begin to crumble and our mental health deteriorates. Without habits, we are thrown out of our usual groove of behavioral consistency.

Human beings are creatures of habit. Experts tell us that sticking to routines and rituals and performing repetitive tasks helps us predict outcomes more accurately. And, by the way, they also reduce stress and soothe our fear of uncertainty. Believe it or not, there is psychological value in regularly performing commonplace duties such as throwing out the trash, tidying up your living room, flossing your teeth, and even helping your children do their homework. For example, if you floss regularly, perhaps you won't lose your teeth and look unattractive to others. If you consistently throw out your trash, perhaps you are safeguarding your home from harmful germs or even disease. Journalist Kate Murphy said, "But it's mundane routines that give us structure to help us pare things down and better navigate the world, which helps us make sense of things and feel that life has meaning."[2]

> STICKING TO ROUTINES AND RITUALS AND PERFORMING REPETITIVE TASKS HELPS US PREDICT OUTCOMES MORE ACCURATELY.

Predicting outcomes has obvious benefit because by engaging in this type of statistical foreshadowing over the ages, we have learned to bolster ourselves from potential dangers. For instance, if suddenly our lives are disrupted and we can't complete steadfast daily routines the way we typically do, there's a problem. "If you can't do it the way you normally do, you're biologically engineered to get upset," said Murphy.

BE OPEN TO A NEW DIRECTION

Nostalgia and daydreaming are keys to the grief experience because they open up in us the possibility of a new direction in our immediate future. They use the past to help shape us into something new for the road ahead. Nostalgia and daydreaming also help us with creativity, goal-setting, problem-solving, and, sometimes, just pure positive escapism. What if we were able to draw an imaginary line in the sand and see ourselves at a crossroads of personal change? A new intersection that includes the practice of positive nostalgia as well as healthy daydreaming for a better future?

Building resilience starts with intention. Taking cues from our daydreams, habits, and nostalgia, we can create intention to establish, reestablish, or cultivate new behavioral consistencies. Or we can return to the previous ones that gave us structure and meaning in our lives. But let's also consider launching brand-new practices and personal customs within the settings that we find ourelves in, whether at home or in the workplace. We can focus on finding routines that involve structure and tasks that stimulate our minds.

It's natural for us to get so attached to how things were that we fail to open up to new habits and behaviors. We fail to adapt to change. We become sedentary. Perchance the time has come to create a "new self" of intent. A new self that positively embraces all experiences from the past—even the painful ones that caused us suffering—and perhaps is not afraid of engaging in some optimistic dreaming.

In the end, we cannot control what happens to us, but we can and should try to positively launch new habits that give our lives a secure base. This assists our brains in developing a healthier outlook and being more prepared for what life throws at us. And there will always be new upheavals to grapple with—the question is not how, but when.

ROMANTIC HOPEFULNESS

As we have discussed in this book, rousing music, or any art form for that matter, stimulates hopefulness. That's why having your go-to art medium nearby to inspire nostalgia is so important. And if it stimulates healthy daydreaming, that's also a plus.

Romantic composer Robert Schumann's 1838 *Kinderszenen* Opus 15 ("Scenes from Childhood"), also known as *Träumerie* ("Dreaming"), is the quintessential romantic excursion into the human daydream. *Träumerie* is a contemplative, moving piece, dripping with pensive bittersweetness. Schumann's composition fills the senses with romantic wistfulness, and

THE MAGIC IN THE TRAGIC

even when we listen to it for the first time, it feels like a retrospective transport into a time when our lives were simple, innocent, idealistic. His small-form compositions, also known as piano miniatures, were considered impetuous, fanciful, and lyrical, yet they cut deep into the psyche with an air of crushing tragedy, said Phil G. Goulding in his book compilation, *Classical Music: 50 Great Composers and Their 1,000 Greatest Works*. One critic wrote, "No composer has whispered such secrets of subtle and ravishing beauty to a receptive listener."[3]

Schumann seemed to have suffered from severe mental illness ranging from today's bipolar disorder (mania) to severe depression and even psychosis. He also appeared to have developed acute paranoia and suffered delusions of being poisoned. He attempted suicide in 1854 and then admitted himself to a hospital in Bonn, Germany. He was considered the most romantic of the romantic composers because even during his gravest bouts of mental disturbance, he was still prolific. He died two years later of pneumonia at age forty-six.[4]

The essence of Schumann's story is that despite his mental health condition, like Van Gogh and many other artists, his mesmerizing compositions demonstrate how the power of art can transcend any affliction, even mental illness. More importantly, they show how art can positively fill our minds with anticipation and hope.

TRY THIS PRACTICE

Schedule Daydreaming Moments

Once per day, take a quick break from your everyday activities and listen to a musical piece of your choosing, gaze at artwork that inspires you, or visit a setting in nature that you love. Anything of your choosing that helps you get out of your surface thinking for a moment.

As you engage, pay attention to the daydreamlike places your mind goes to. It could conjure a memorable time in your recent or distant past that was meaningful to you. Or it could be something you are looking forward to or hoping for in the near future. Let your imagination wander freely, and try not to judge it or qualify it in any way. Whatever images arise will be right.

Your daydreams might also be recollections, hopes, or aspirations you have kept secret for years due to fear of ridicule. Or memories or expectations you have avoided because you were afraid of what feelings they would bring up. Your daydreams could involve considering a different career, traveling to a destination you always wanted to visit, planning for the future, or fulfilling a bucket-list activity you have sidestepped for years, or they could be as simple as recalling important people in your life whom you miss.

CHAPTER 11

THE IMPORTANCE OF EMOTIONAL VULNERABILITY

How to Build Self-Compassion

Self-love is learning how to listen to your own heart so you can understand someone else's.

ZELLA SAGE

THE UNIVERSAL YEARNING FOR HUMAN BELONGING IS A PRE-vailing force. It holds us together like the massive power of gravity keeps the celestial bodies in our solar system from straying off their orbits and causing interplanetary confusion. And even though ambition, achievement, money, security,

THE MAGIC IN THE TRAGIC

faith, and the many other things that guide us are important, the ideal we all seek is embedded in the quality and depth of our human connections and our ability to be vulnerable with one another. Humans are wired for connection.

But our American society doesn't always think so. We still covet the ethos of independence and individualism instead of interdependence and having commonality with others. Unlike other countries, the "collective" is not as important as the separate self. In this country, grit and distinctiveness are praised as virtues and the concept of vulnerability gets blurred. Somehow being vulnerable gets mixed up with appearing needy or weak. We are praised for our ability to stand on our own, and people avoid asking for assistance at all costs.

> GRIT AND DISTINCTIVENESS ARE PRAISED AS VIRTUES AND THE CONCEPT OF VULNERABILITY GETS BLURRED.

To combat our society's individualistic tendencies, we need to actively work toward interdependence and vulnerability. Author Alissa Quart talked about the benefits of practicing being dependent on others. Quart called it the "art of dependence." She defined it as "accepting aid with grace and, crucially, recognizing the importance in others—and even on the state. It takes dignity and skill to lean on friends, loved ones, and colleagues. Resourcefulness is required for collaboration."[1] If humans are indeed programmed to prioritize togetherness, not acknowledging the importance of others and not practicing the skill of vulnerability means we are going against the natural order of things.

THE IMPORTANCE OF EMOTIONAL VULNERABILITY

ACCEPTING VULNERABILITY MAKES US MORE RESILIENT

Arthur Schopenhauer, well known for his atheistic and pessimistic beliefs, was, in fact, a robust advocate of human connection as the only tangible deliverance from a bleak life. He believed that because all of life is suffering, our *raison d'être* is to huddle together as best we can and comfort one another along the way. Without one another, we would perish. In an essay called *On the Sufferings of the World*, published in 1851, he discussed the idea that tragedy and suffering add to the breadth of connectivity, and, through the unity of that suffering and the shared vulnerability, we are inescapably linked to one another.[2] He went further to embrace the omnipresence of suffering by suggesting the following:

> From this point of view, one might indeed consider that the appropriate form of address between man and man ought to be, not *monsieur, sir*, but *fellow sufferer, compagnon de misères*. However strange this may sound it corresponds to the nature of the case, makes us see other men in a true light and reminds us of what are the most necessary of all things: tolerance, patience, forbearance and charity, which each of us needs and which each of us therefore owes.[3]

While "fellow sufferer" might seem a little dramatic in this day and age, there is value in the term. I see a reverent equitability to it, a leveling of the playing field of humanity. In many ways, if we *did* see one another as human beings who are equally susceptible to the same conditions of pain and suffering, I think there would be a greater sense of mutual respect and harmony in the world.

In his book *The Wisdom of Insecurity*, English writer and philosopher Alan Watts spoke eloquently about pain and human frailty: "By all outward appearances our life is a spark of light between one eternal darkness and another. Nor is the interval between these two nights an unclouded day, for the more we are able to feel pleasure, the more we are vulnerable to pain—and whether in background or foreground, the pain is always with us."[4] If the "pain is always with us," so is the emotional vulnerability. The longing for love, friendship, connection, compassion, security, safety, and health is in our DNA. Accepting our vulnerability makes us all feel less alone. Knowing the quiet poise and inner peace of that knowledge builds emotional resilience, and so does, as mentioned in earlier chapters, espousing constructive aching and allowing ourselves to experience positive wounding.

ACCEPTING IMPERFECTIONS INSTEAD OF FAILURE

Recently, no one has done more research on the subject of vulnerability than author Brené Brown. She believes vulnerability is integrating and embracing our imperfections *and* knowing we matter and belong as well. She believes that accessing

THE IMPORTANCE OF EMOTIONAL VULNERABILITY

vulnerability is a way to heighten awareness to our fears that block our ability to be genuine with others. In her book *Daring Greatly*, she wrote, "Vulnerability is the birthplace of love, belonging, joy, courage, empathy and creativity. It is the source of hope, empathy, accountability and authenticity."[5]

Being vulnerable is perhaps one of the most important emotions we need in order to stay resilient. The benefits are tenfold. Imagine how powerful we could be if we removed emotional obstacles that stop us from living up to our full potential—worries and trepidations that we are not "good enough" or that we are undeserving of love. But most central is experiencing connection with others. Because if we were all joined by the beauty of imperfection, we would be happier and more successful, and we would help one another move forward in the future.

> BEING VULNERABLE IS PERHAPS ONE OF THE MOST IMPORTANT EMOTIONS WE NEED IN ORDER TO STAY RESILIENT.

Underneath the vulnerability there is fear, and to face it, to evolve from it, we must practice being vulnerable. Otherwise, we will remain slaves of our chronic preoccupation with rejection and failure. One way to practice this and help reduce the fear is to allow ourselves to accept our fallibilities. Author Beth Kempton told us that "revealing our vulnerabilities, challenges, as-yet-unrealized dreams, and quirky joys opens a window into our hearts."[6]

As discussed in chapter 6, fear drives our aversion to looking vulnerable. Fear thrives on ambiguity and the potential negative assessments from other people. When we fear being deleteriously evaluated by others, what *actually* distresses us is a kind of social phobia that suggests once people *really* get to know who we are, they will not like us—and in time, they will reject us.

For many people with a social phobia, what we fear most is being publicly exposed and humiliated. Ellen Hendriksen, PhD, author of *How to Be Yourself*,[7] called it the "reveal." The highly undesirable shock of getting publicly "found out" for what we are most ashamed of—the big secret of our imagined inadequacies, our weaknesses and incompetencies. "Ultimately, social anxiety is the fear that whatever we're trying to hide will be revealed to everyone like a gust of wind sweeps away a bad toupee. We *think* there is something wrong with us and therefore try to conceal it."[8]

The "reveal" may also include things that we have done in the past that we are embarrassed about. Perhaps things we missed out on, or things we neglected, or behaviors we engaged in that we are self-conscious about. Social phobia even makes us worry about just *appearing* anxious in the company of others, like if we are sweating, or our cheeks flush, or if we stumble with our words or we think we don't have anything interesting to say. All these responses to social situations are knee-jerk reactions to cover up the illusory inferiority. "Put another way, social anxiety is about concealment. It's less about fear and more about shame, a word that can be traced to the Indo-European root *skam*, meaning "to cover." In short, shame makes us want to hide," said Hendriksen.[9]

THE IMPORTANCE OF EMOTIONAL VULNERABILITY

WHAT IS TOXIC SHAME?

There are many different types of shame. For example, there are instances of "shame-lite" that occur in our lives every day. There's the shame we feel when we absentmindedly trip on the sidewalk while walking on a public street. We wonder if anyone saw how silly or clumsy we look. Or a friend quietly whispers to us at a restaurant that we have a speck of green lettuce stuck in between our teeth and we think how ugly and unattractive that is. Both instances are mildly unsettling for most people, but embarrassing nonetheless. We can safely say that the discomfort we feel in those situations comes from the well of healthy shame—the kind of mild indignity we need to help us stay in line with social norms, proper behavior, and appearance etiquette. The kind of appearance etiquette that forces us to put clothes on every morning and not walk in the streets naked.

Then there is "toxic shame," the chronic and debilitating shame that fools us into thinking we are irreversibly defective. It's the persistent and unyielding sense that no matter what we do, or do *not* do, in this life, deep down inside, we are unworthy of compassion. We feel so much indignity about who we are that if we fall short of perfection, we see ourselves as beneath contempt and beyond forgiveness. It's a classic *organizing principle* that I have discussed in this book—unverified and abstract beliefs about ourselves that are not based in reality. These beliefs are mainly conceived in our own minds, and over the years have grown into factual data. As a result, we don't see our true "self" anymore. We see a deficient illusion of it.

Toxic shame, according to author and educator John Bradshaw, is the biggest obstacle to being connected to others in relationships.[10] It destroys lives by affecting our self-esteem and our confidence. It causes anxiety and depression, and increases the chances of developing substance abuse problems. In Bradshaw's groundbreaking book, *Healing the Shame that Binds You*, he said that he believes that toxic shame erodes your sense of self-worth, leaving you feeling unworthy of love and respect from others.

> TOXIC SHAME IS THE BIGGEST OBSTACLE TO BEING CONNECTED TO OTHERS IN RELATIONSHIPS.

Embracing our vulnerability is the antidote to the deceptive specter of the "reveal" and to toxic shame. How do we apply the remedy? We start with learning about self-compassion.

EXERCISING SELF-COMPASSION

There are things we can do to remind ourselves that we can get better and move forward. Self-compassion begets self-confidence, which ultimately helps us to be proud of ourselves despite what we've been through.

We always hear about how exercising compassion for others and being of service can be healing and transformative. It promotes happiness, helps with stress relief, reduces symptoms of depression, and so much more.[11] When you

THE IMPORTANCE OF EMOTIONAL VULNERABILITY

exercise compassion for others, you can't go wrong. It's a win-win situation. But what about exercising *self*-compassion? It's just as important because to be a compassionate and giving person, we must feel and experience that same humanity for ourselves. Having compassion for ourselves affects every area of our lives. To be happy and live a fulfilling life, we need to feel good about who we are and what we are doing. "Compassion for yourself is where you start when things are tough, not where you stop," said Rick Hanson. "Self-compassion makes a person more resilient, more able to bounce back. It lowers self-criticism and builds up self-worth."[12]

But to achieve this self-assurance, we must practice it. We need to be mindfully aware of how we see ourselves, how we relate to others, and how we view the world as a whole. Sounds simple, but it's not. For some of us, giving ourselves a break, even once in a while, is actually difficult to do. Why is that?

Perhaps over the years we have unknowingly etched into our minds a template of disapproval about ourselves—an indelible image of unworthiness. As discussed earlier, organizing principles are the blueprints of our inner dialogue. Sometimes that inner dialogue is so powerful, we call it fate. A good example of an organizing principle around shame might be: *I am different; therefore, I am unworthy of compassion.*

If I believe that about myself, my view of the future and of the world is colored by this biased view of myself. Another example is when we conclude that because our careers, business ventures, or relationships have not gone exactly our way, we are failures for not living up to certain expectations. Or when we instinctively deprive ourselves of consideration while going through a difficult time with a mental health condition, or a chronic illness, or a life event. Others get a hall pass or a get-out-of-jail-free card. But we don't.

Researcher, author, and professor Dr. Kristin Neff studies how we learn and practice self-compassion. One of the ways she defined self-compassion is to be gentle with ourselves and choose kindness instead of constantly judging ourselves for our mistakes and faults. By changing the way we treat ourselves, we establish a consistent type of emotional stability that can always be built on. Accessing self-compassion is like installing shock absorbers to cushion us from negative feelings of shame, inadequacy, and fear.

Recognizing self-compassion as a shielding influence is crucial to understanding ourselves because the mind is not designed to focus on the positives. "Our brains evolved to be highly sensitive to negative information so that the fight-or-flight response could be triggered quickly and easily in the brain's amygdala," according to Neff in her book *Self-Compassion: The Proven Power of Being Yourself.*[13] As discussed in chapter 9, because the brain's smoke detector—the threat response—is fail-safe, we are instead compelled to pay more attention to the negatives in order to preserve the human organism. Whether we are a fight, flight, or even a freeze responder, dwelling on positives is not in our nature.

The bad news about that is we tend to overlook our positives because neurobiologically they are not essential for future survival. But are they? If Neff's work is effective,

THE IMPORTANCE OF EMOTIONAL VULNERABILITY

perhaps the human mind can evolve by altering the neurochemistry of how we respond to negative stimuli. If we can change the way we react to trauma, we can also transform the way we process shame. Learning self-compassion is a game-changer because we don't have to rely on anyone to give it to us. We can really become our own electrician and independently rewire our brains for self-kindness. If we suffer from shame, self-loathing, and inadequacy, or another mental health condition—or even if we don't—it's incumbent upon us to take action and nurture the power of self-compassion.

> LEARNING SELF-COMPASSION IS A GAME-CHANGER BECAUSE WE DON'T HAVE TO RELY ON ANYONE TO GIVE IT TO US.

A MODERN-DAY STOIC

English musician Matt Johnson, formerly of the eighties post-punk band The The, has always owned a profound respect for his unyielding shame and vulnerability. Johnson writes introspective, relatable, thought-provoking songs that focus on the human plight of being fallible and imperfect, from selfishness, to lamenting a regrettable past, to being haunted by lost love, to fixating on death. However, Johnson does not beseech us for pity. Like the ancient stoics, he holds himself accountable for all the reckless choices he's made and for the unavoidable fickleness of life that we are all susceptible to.

Johnson's clever lyrics and catchy melodies temper the

unavoidable reality of human vulnerability with honorable tenderness. In his 1993 song "Lonely Planet,"[14] he sang about never being able to skirt accountability in life despite his self-inflicted shame. Toward the end of the song, Johnson offered advice for building emotional resilience.

> ANOTHER WAY OF BUILDING SELF-COMPASSION IS TO ACKNOWLEDGE THAT EVERYONE'S PATH IS DIFFERENT.

To Johnson, perhaps another way of building self-compassion is to acknowledge that everyone's path is different. Hence, if you feel that "changing your world"—a much more difficult thing to do than changing yourself—is more your speed, go for it. No judgment. But do it confidently and earnestly.

TRY THIS PRACTICE

Cultivating Self-Compassion

Here are a few steps to cultivating self-compassion regardless of whether you struggle with mental health issues or not. As we work toward emotional resiliency and more vulnerability, self-compassion will be key to the process.

1. Kindness

Kindness to yourself involves being wholehearted and empathetic toward yourself whenever you are feeling inadequate, alone, depressed, or anxious. You can choose to be on your own side and support yourself unconditionally. It won't come easy at first. For many, the knee-jerk reaction when faced with any kind of adversity is to deprive yourself of any empathy and to blame yourself. But this exercise asks you to try something new and choose kindness over disapproval. Remember, no one can give you the level of effective kindness and compassion that you can provide for yourself.

> **Task:** List five ways you offered kindness to someone else in the recent past. Keep the list handy and review it regularly to remember that you are also deserving of the same level of kindness.

2. Focus on Your Strengths

We all possess strengths. What are yours? Consciously zero in on the things you know you are good at. This will help you define yourself by these strengths, not by your imagined shortcomings. It's also important to stop comparing yourself to others. No one is like you, and you are not like anybody else. That alone is a strength. That is your superpower. If you base your self-esteem on how well you measure up against your peers, the comparison will never end, because in your mind, you will always find someone out there who is better. Let's instead focus on what you offer the world.

> **Task:** List five strengths you possess. Keep the list handy and review it regularly as your new guiding principles. In time, you will feel your self-confidence improve and your self-compassion increase.

3. Align Yourself with Your Core Values

We all possess core values that drive our existence and are part of the very fabric of who we are as individuals. They give us meaning and a sense of identity. These are things like the love of your family, a friendship you cherish, your faith in God or a higher power, your ability to be creative, your commitment to good health, your self-respect, your love of music, and so on. Over the years, our core values tend to be neglected or put aside. As a result, our self-confidence takes a big hit because we have lost our sense of direction. If we align our thoughts, behaviors, and actions with our core values, we will feel better about the direction we are going in life right now and will know where to put our energy.

> **Task:** List five personal values that give your life meaning. Keep the list handy and review it regularly.

4. Embrace Your Mistakes

Exercising a daily practice of self-compassion requires learning how to forgive yourself. Whatever mistakes you've made are all part of being human. You probably did the best you could at the time, and you have been punishing yourself about it ever since. As a result, you have deemed yourself unworthy and undeserving of forgiveness and ultimately compassion. Instead, see your mistakes as learning experiences. Consider looking at them as potential breakthroughs instead of breakdowns, as springboards instead of setbacks. In other words, rewrite the script and look at any mistake or shortcoming as a teacher, a learning tool to help you improve your life.

> **Task:** List five people you admire and respect who've made mistakes but have found forgiveness. Keep the list handy and review it regularly to remember that you are human and deserve forgiveness too.

5. Be Proud of Who You Are

Learn to appreciate your individuality and who you are. Don't be so preoccupied with what others think of you, and don't make others the keepers of your self-esteem.

Most people are not worrying or thinking about you as much as you think they are, so you don't need to give them that power. Your opinion of yourself is the only one that matters. Choose compassionate ways to think about yourself, like, *I am a survivor.* Or *I am only human*, or *I am doing the best I can every day.*

>**Task:** List five things you like about yourself. Keep the list handy and review it regularly to be mindful of what you are most proud of about yourself.

6. Be Aware of Your Emotional Blind Spots

Try to be your own therapist and notice the patterns of emotional reactivity in your life. Notice where your blind spots are—the things in your life that cause you to not think clearly because you are either scared, hurt, or angry. Do your emotions flare up in an irrational or unstable way in social settings? When speaking face-to-face with a superior? When talking to a loved one you are in conflict with? Knowing what your blind spots are and then being mindful of them will help you feel more balanced when faced with emotional adversity. You will be combat ready for whatever comes your way.

And you will be able to build self-compassion because the more familiar you are with who you are and what makes you tick, the more respectful you will be toward yourself. In other words, by giving your blind spots some acceptance, you won't be so harsh with yourself in the future. You will gradually begin to accept and integrate all aspects of your personality.

Task: List five personal blind spots that trigger emotionality. Keep the list handy and review it regularly to be mindful of these vulnerable and sensitive situations.

Practicing these six tips regularly will not only increase your self-compassion and self-confidence, but it will also create abundance for you and for everyone you encounter. Rick Hanson said, "Getting on your own side and bringing caring to your pain will make you more resilient, confident, and capable. Being good to yourself is good for others too."[15] Human compassion is the eighth wonder of the world because it's not hierarchical, it's reciprocal. It has the ability to validate, not separate, and, most importantly, to normalize, not stigmatize.

If all of us engage in self-compassion practice, we are helping shape an unshakable core of veracity. If we are kinder to ourselves, the world will follow.

CHAPTER 12

LEARNING TO LIVE LIKE THE OCEAN

Going with the Flow

*Be a Columbus to whole new continents
and worlds within you, opening new
channels, not of trade, but of thought.*

HENRY DAVID THOREAU

WHEN WE FEEL WE ARE LOSING CONTROL OVER OUR LIVES OR when an unstable world makes us feel like the earth is shifting beneath our feet, we reach for anything in a feeble attempt to stabilize the situation. That *anything* is usually something already familiar to us—like an old survival mechanism that has become less effective over the years. As a result, we are unable to shed any new light on our dilemma because we never consider questioning the "knowns" of our mental processing. Our personal knowns sometimes prevent us from

THE MAGIC IN THE TRAGIC

letting go or relaxing. It can feel like we're spinning our wheels but upside down.

The reality is, we need to challenge our "fixed" thinking and be curious about the "knowns" all over again. By hacking into our former system's programs and defamiliarizing ourselves with the familiar, we can cultivate new coping skills.

From his poem "Good Advice for Someone Like Me," the late folk singer Leonard Cohen poetically wrote, "If you don't become the ocean, you'll be seasick every day."[1] In this metaphor, he compared the existence of being human to an erratic, unpredictable ocean. Living like the ocean is anything but "fixed" or familiar.

If we don't learn to live like the ocean with all its chaotic variability, we suffer. The ocean's mighty swells, deadly currents, frightening depths, its grandeur and even mystery fascinate us, but also scare us. So it is with life and all its unpredictable highs and lows. As we all know, life can be unsteady, frightening, and super difficult if we don't learn to go with the flow. We may desperately want permanence and guarantees, but that is just not reality.

> IF WE DON'T LEARN TO LIVE LIKE THE OCEAN WITH ALL ITS CHAOTIC VARIABILITY, WE SUFFER.

We fight against the power of the ocean, the hardships of life, and this makes our distress and grief worse. We create an inner hell of intolerance, impatience, worry, anger, resentment, and fear of change. Although we sometimes realize that these old methods don't help us anymore, even still we do them over and over again.

One of the problems is that we wish life could always be easy and happy, like a calm and tranquil ocean that never changes. That delusion causes us suffering. "Becoming like the ocean" means we aren't so attached to happiness. It means we accept that it won't always be smooth sailing. However, if we choose, we can learn how not to be averse to adverse events. We just need to find our sea legs.

CHANGING YOUR FIXED THINKING: BE YOUR OWN HAMLET

One way to be like the ocean and to challenge fixed thinking is to become the master of your destiny. A great classical reference for this is Hamlet. In Henry Douglas Wild's book, *Shakespeare: Prophet for Our Time*, he offered the proposition of becoming your own Hamlet as a way to build resilience: "to be one's own Hamlet . . . is thus to embark upon an expedition into oneself in a manner as simple and direct as it is profound."[2]

After Hamlet's father, the king of Denmark, is murdered, his ghost appears and tells his young son to avenge his death against his uncle Claudius.[3] The unsteady Hamlet has to also contend with the news that his mother, Gertrude, who quickly married Claudius after the murder, is complicit in the crime. Hamlet's world is shattered and turned upside down. The iconic query "to be or not to be" conveys his questioning of whether to remain idle or to see justice served for his father.[4]

"To be" and to achieve his goal, the fledgling prince Hamlet has to defamiliarize himself with his loyal beliefs in the integrity of the Danish throne. He must let go of his fixed "knowns" and believe not only in the supernatural ghost of his father, but in the fact that family corruption has infiltrated what is sacred to him. He must also accept the tragic realization that his beloved mother is an accomplice in the assassination. But, despite his fear and hesitancy, he eventually chooses to act. He refuses to become victim of the "slings and arrows of outrageous fortune" and instead decides to live like the ocean and "take arms against a sea of troubles."[5] The wisdom in Shakespeare's timeless play is a reflection of the growth and personal integration we attain when we ourselves decide to be the architects of our life path.

GOING WITH THE FLOW: BE LIKE FORREST GUMP

Or, if Hamlet is not for you and being the master of your destiny sounds terrifying, be your own Forrest Gump. If there was ever a character who knew how best to "go with the flow," it's Forrest Gump. Wherever the wind blew him and wherever he ended up, that's where he was. He accepted it without question. But every situation that fate put him in, he also excelled in. He is the most heroic antihero of all time. So perhaps there is value in allowing fate to be in charge.

Gump, played masterfully by Tom Hanks in the 1994 film, was not the brooding, troubled, and analytical hero like Shakespeare's Hamlet. Gump was instead a dry, deadpan commoner with a low IQ whose charm lay in his honorable naivete. His out-of-touch presence with the social intricacies and innuendos of life didn't affect him. But, within his innocence was an almost messiah-like aura because of his uncritical and nonjudgmental perception of all people and his ability to see the good in everything. Throughout the film, everybody who meets Forrest is better for it in the end.

Unlike Hamlet's dilemma, Gump's decisions and actions are based on very little reasoning and more on impulse. Luckily for him, his impulses were always proper and moral. To him life was truly like a "box of chocolates" because when you don't have a preconceived purpose in life and you're not put in a position of leadership, life can sway you in any direction. Gump was not the architect of his destiny; however, the beauty of the film is that if we allow the universe to guide us, sometimes good things happen. Gump lived like the ocean, even if he was unaware of it.[6]

OPENING NEW CHANNELS OF THOUGHT AND BEHAVIOR

Our ability to shift gears and open our minds to the unfamiliar is important to our success as a species. Not only for huge crises or natural disasters, but for our own personal challenges and losses to come. Our ability to change the way we look at things might insulate us from the next catastrophe.

In my experience as a treating psychotherapist, the individuals I have seen who achieve the most improvement in their distress are those who are willing to change their behaviors. Everyone comes to therapy with good intentions, but having the will to get better isn't always enough. When we can focus on ourselves as opposed to focusing on the externals, we increase our chances of success because we endow ourselves with self-empowerment. Hence, *we* are in command. Plus, the only thing we *do* have control over in this life is ourselves.

How do we help ourselves change in our behaviors? Easier said than done. The truth is, it can be hard to alter any behavior that has not been serving us well. Trying to stop anything cold turkey that we are accustomed to will fail, and perhaps it has already many times. But if we play the game of inches and create a gradual process, beginning with small, incremental behavioral goals that are achievable—minuscule as they might be—we will feel encouraged and inspired to go further. The new behavior change will open the new channels of thought too. If we look at the new behavior as an expedition, an adventure to a new world of relating to our lives, there is no limit to what we can achieve.

> IF WE LOOK AT THE NEW BEHAVIOR AS AN EXPEDITION, AN ADVENTURE TO A NEW WORLD OF RELATING TO OUR LIVES, THERE IS NO LIMIT TO WHAT WE CAN ACHIEVE.

LEARNING TO LIVE LIKE THE OCEAN

CHANGING BEHAVIORS: DAMIEN'S STORY

Years ago, I worked with a forty-six-year-old patient named Damien, who suffered from a moderate to severe case of obsessive-compulsive disorder (OCD). He was dealing with many existential issues regarding his career, his purpose in life, and marital problems. He had two children and lived in a quiet suburb outside of Los Angeles.

His biggest fear was failing to measure up to his high expectations as a top executive at a prominent financial planning firm. As a result, Damien spent most of his days worrying about being ousted by the board of directors. He expended a great deal of time checking, rechecking, and triple checking outgoing emails for errors. After having meetings or personal conversations with his staff and colleagues, he would mentally review the conversations in his head repeatedly to make sure he hadn't said anything inappropriate. And on a regular basis he persistently questioned his performance and his productivity at the company. He also worried about his volatile temper, which was often unleashed on his young staff. He felt guilty about being too tough on them for not working as hard as he did.

If Damien felt he exceeded expectations during a particular week and his staff made him look good by doing the same, he was happy. If he didn't (in his mind), his job was in jeopardy. The problem was, he rarely felt good about his performance or his staff's. Damien came to me on the verge of not only quitting his job but considering leaving the finance industry altogether. He worried he was not cut out for it and wasn't cut out for being a boss. He once said, "Maybe I wasn't meant to be a leader." He was ready to throw in the towel.

I worked with Damien to cognitively restructure his thinking around his high demands for absolute excellence. But he still couldn't stop the negative behaviors of chronically second-guessing himself, checking, seeking reassurance, and berating his staff. Despite changing his viewpoint and reducing some of his anxiety, he was still engaging in the same time-consuming "checking" behaviors that were detrimental to him. The behaviors were taking up way too much of the day and ironically hurting his performance at work even more.

What I asked Damien to do felt impossible to him at first. He thought I was being ridiculous. Because I couldn't ask him to simply stop the reassurance-seeking behavior, I instead asked him to first delay his compulsion instead of immediately engaging in it every single time he had the urge. For instance, the moment he felt triggered to begin the checking protocol with his emails, I asked him to delay the onset of the protocol for one minute. Then after the minute was up, he could go right ahead and check. Eventually the one-minute exposure got extended to five minutes, then ten minutes, and so on. The delay in checking, even for one minute, allowed him to slowly learn to endure the discomfort of *not* checking. He had never given himself that opportunity to feel the fear, hence he avoided the pain every single time. This led to him being a slave to the checking and to the imperfections of his staff.

Another technique to modify his behavior was to alter the frequency of the behavior. After the delay, if he checked his outgoing emails five times before hitting the send button, I would ask him to reread it only four times. If the entire reassurance-seeking timeframe took twenty minutes out of his day, I would ask him to only spend seventeen minutes of time on it, each time decreasing the frequency of the behavior.

Every week the goal was to gradually reduce the timeframe and reduce the number of rechecking cycles he implemented. The goals we set each week were easily measurable, and, most importantly, they were achievable. When he started to notice that he was doing the behavior a little bit less, although the anxiety of missing an error and not getting the reassurance he needed scared him, it made him feel better. Eventually, the checking frequency dropped to one time for every composed email. The duration lasted less than two minutes.

I'll add that during the delay time before the checking compulsion, I asked him to practice deactivating the threat response in the moment by engaging in 4–7–8 breathing, tension and release, and repeating affirmations. This gave him something to ground himself with as he endured the discomfort of delaying his compulsion.

As mentioned, Damien naturally found my treatment plan outrageous because he feared that by delaying and later skipping the familiar steps of his "known" coping skill, he would be left vulnerable to mistakes. But the ups and downs of his work culture in finance caused him to be seasick every day. Living like the ocean and going with the flow was a concept he could not grasp at first. But steadily, via exposure to the discomfort, the delay tactics allowed him to feel the fear before reaching for what he knew, which was to try and control the possibility of making an error. Damien first had to accept that the old ways of getting through the day and preserving his career were a hindrance. He had to change the way he related to his job instead of quitting his job. He finished treatment with a more resilient sense of resolve about himself. The changes he saw elevated his confidence. The treatment also humbled his unrealistic and dogged determination to be impossibly perfect all the time.

CREATING GOOD KARMA

I hope that by this point you have acclimatized yourself to the everyday awareness of the instructive and poetic beauty that surrounds us. By now, your commitment to opening your mind to *inspiration exposure*, whether through music, literature, art, philosophy, nature, or any medium that moves you, should be budding.

> "EXPERIENCE IS NOT WHAT HAPPENS TO A MAN; IT IS WHAT A MAN DOES WITH WHAT HAPPENS TO HIM."

Aldous Huxley famously opined, "Experience is not what happens to a man; it is what a man does with what happens to him."[7] It's incumbent upon us to insulate ourselves from future loss and the next natural disaster with the *magic in the tragic* tools discussed in this book. These tools of awareness are the building blocks for fortifying ourselves with emotional resilience.

Committing to the practice of converting our tragic into magic is what karma is all about. *Karma*, from the Sanskrit word meaning "act,"[8] is about how we can influence the future with our actions. Karma is not an invisible force generated by the universe that has power over our destiny. Who creates the karma? We do. We do it with our actions, with our thoughts. We create it by how we deal with pain and suffering too. The karma we choose is up to us.

Hence, instead of allowing life to treat us as victims, we can take the bull of suffering by the horns and create our own intention. Like young Prince Hamlet taking "arms against the sea of troubles,"[9] we are confronted with these dilemmas every single minute of the day. Aging, illness, and death are unavoidable. Even with our everyday worries, fears, and disappointments, we have the option to respond differently. We can adopt a new attitude and perception of suffering. We can find the dignity in suffering and ennoble our pain.

LIVE! LIVE!

In the 1971 black comedy *Harold and Maude*, Harold, played by Bud Cort, is a lonely, depressed young man who's obsessed with death. He is not afraid of dying per se; rather, he is afraid of living. He spends much of his days imagining creative ways to end his life. Harold is a suffering misfit who has given up

THE MAGIC IN THE TRAGIC

on love, people, and human connection. He has no friends and no interests other than his preoccupation with the macabre.

Throughout the first quarter of the film, we see Harold play-acting inventive methods of committing suicide intended, presumably, to get a rise out of his emotionally detached mother who pays little attention to him. His staged demises are elaborate and gruesomely funny.

Maude, portrayed by the hilarious Ruth Gordon, is a piss-and-vinegar, seventy-nine-year-old eccentric who befriends Harold after meeting him at a random funeral (a gloomy voyeuristic activity they both happen to enjoy). Their complementary, morbid inclinations lead them to engage in an improbable romance that is heartwarming despite their sixty-year age gap. Maude cooks for him, teaches him about music, and they have picnics at cemeteries and go on road trips to rescue trees suffocating in big cities.

Eventually, Maude teaches Harold how to develop sea legs and embrace his pain. She helps him mend his broken spirit and shows him the beauty and magic in life, despite its often tragic nature. Harold learns that the brief pockets of joy within all the sadness he has been running from are worth living for. Essentially, she saves his life by altering his fixed experience of grief into *constructive aching* and *positive wounding*. "Harold," she advises him, "reach out. Take a chance. Get hurt even. But play as well as you can. Go team, go! . . . L-i-v-e! Live! Otherwise, you got nothing to talk about in the locker room."

On her eightieth birthday, after Maude feels she has satisfactorily mentored her young student and is confident that Harold is ready to reconnect to life again, she confesses that she swallowed fatal pills an hour earlier. "I'll be gone by midnight."

"What?!" Harold screams in shock. He rushes her to the emergency room, hoping to reverse the lethal potion she has ingested. In the end, it's too late.

Yet, despite the utter terror of losing the only friend he's ever had, Harold accepts that Maude's time has come. Tearful and inconsolable, he chooses not to end his life as he originally intended before he fell in love with Maude. He decides to go on with his life and practice the legacy of living like the ocean. Although the tragedy of her loss is devastating, the magnitude of the pain is diminished because Maude helped him discover the value in finding the magic in the tragic.[10]

Like Maude, I also choose to engulf myself with all the grandeur I can find, and it doesn't only have to be through the sublime province of the arts. It can be through connections with other people, through inspiration from work and career, or from spending time in nature. It could be so many different things, so long as it alters my consciousness and allows me to experience the magic in my life. Age and stage of life don't matter either. Maybe you're just starting out in your life journey as a young adult, or are in midlife, or coming to the tail end of it. Noticing the many enchantments that make your existence splendorous is the bedrock of emotional resilience.[11]

TRY THIS PRACTICE

Creating Good Karma

The Book of Awesome by Neil Pasricha is a brilliant collection of plain, everyday things we forget to notice and appreciate in our daily lives. Each lighthearted chapter prompts us to draw attention to tiny, awesome aspects of being human. For example, the author asks us to stop and notice simple pleasures like "nailing a parallel parking attempt on the first try," or enjoying "perfectly popped microwave popcorn."

In the spirit of creating good karma, here's an exercise that will encourage you to cherish the little things in *your* life that sometimes go unnoticed. If each day you take the time to acknowledge life's small gifts, you will be better prepared for difficult days in the future. In a sense you are insulating yourself from adversity and boosting your emotional immune system. Remember, if the cause and effect of our actions creates our destiny, then the sum of these tiny observations today might help us build resilience for tomorrow.

Step 1: Every morning when you wake up, commit to being a keen observer of what you see and feel. Commit to noticing and then documenting small things throughout your day that make you smile. It could be as simple as enjoying that first sip of your morning coffee; it might be hearing an old favorite song on your drive home that elevates your mood, or sneaking in a quick afternoon nap.

Step 2: Once you identify the source of your emotional shift, write it down on a pad of paper or save it on your smartphone. Whether you document one special moment each day or one hundred special moments is up to you. The more the better.

Step 3: Each evening, review the list and think about how great those moments were. Take in the memory of how good you felt when it happened. In other words, re-expose yourself to the joy. The repetition of consistently noticing the good (even if it's minor) will begin to restructure your days. In time, your mind will be primed to single out the positive in your life more frequently. And, even during challenging moments, this exercise might help to brighten your outlook.

FINAL THOUGHTS

GRIEF IS EDUCATION. GRIEF IS KNOWLEDGE. IN BEHAVIORAL psychotherapy, the same way human beings attain the therapeutic milestone of *habituation*—a decrease in response to a stressor after repeated exposure—we can do the same with our feelings of sadness and loss. Habituation means acclimating to the discomfort so the mind starts to tolerate the level of distress better over time. That's why inspiration exposure is the best way to begin this process. Inspiration exposure has the power to transform the pain into a thing of beauty. Every human being at some point in their lives has been favorably moved or touched by meaningful things. You'll do yourself a great service to find those things and keep them by your side as tools for helping you get through any kind of difficulty in the future.

Building emotional resilience is imperative, especially when facing so much uncertainty.

Naturally, when we are confronted with instability and our sense of safety and security are compromised, we lose that optimistic light of awareness and unsuccessfully try to control

FINAL THOUGHTS

things we cannot control. Letting go of undue control may include:

1. **Practicing Acceptance:** Accept that things will not always go as planned on a day-to-day basis. If you expect a bad day every now and then, life will go easier and you will be less disappointed.
2. **Giving Yourself Permission:** Many people believe life should always be easy, happy, cheerful, productive. That's simply unrealistic. Giving yourself permission to actually have a bad day is key. Avoid viewing hard times as personal failures.
3. **Reducing Emotional Reactivity:** Stay grounded by monitoring your emotional reactivity. Otherwise, you will turn into a walking impulse that gets easily unhinged, or you will become irrational over the smallest things and, in the moment, feel like it's the end of the world.

If achieving emotional resilience is important in your life, by now you understand that it *must* coexist as a companion to grief. That doesn't necessarily mean advancing through grief or over it, but more alongside it by finding the poignant and splendid aspects to our pain. Acknowledging the darkness within always helps us ascend to the light. That's why all art forms, as well as the natural beauty that surrounds us, are forms of self-help. Art helps awaken our imaginative side, heal our wounds, and elevate our deepest emotions—even the emotions we often try to avoid.

FINAL THOUGHTS

In May 1976, my family was living in Europe for a brief time, and my seventeen-year-old brother, who was born with weak lungs and suffered severe bouts of asthma throughout his young life, succumbed to his illness and died in a sudden and tragic manner. My parents were devastated. Such a young life taken away so senselessly. My brokenhearted father, who quietly suffered unspeakable sadness, chose to venerate his son's death by building an impressive marble mausoleum and commissioning a painting of him by the well-known American portrait artist Aaron Shikler.

During the funeral, as the congregation moved toward the grave site to lay my brother's body in its final resting place, my father asked a close family friend to lead the trail of mourners while carrying a cassette player and filling the woeful cemetery air with the majestic sound of Richard Wagner's overture to *Tannhäuser*. My father was profoundly moved by Wagner's mythological operatic themes. He was particularly inspired by Wagner's female warriors in Norse mythology—the Valkyries—who were given the sacred trust of recovering heroes fallen in battle and returning them to Valhalla. My brother's funeral was one of the darkest yet most emotionally affecting experiences I've ever witnessed.

For my father, the gallant immortalization of his son was therapeutic. It helped give my brother's death meaning. His intention to valorize the tragedy acted as a unique agent in

FINAL THOUGHTS

transmuting his pain into something glorious. The stately tomb, the distinguished painting, Wagner's overture, and many other attempts to venerate his grief soothed his spirit by balancing out the bereavement with cathartic adulation.

By discovering the dignity in suffering, experiencing the power of constructive aching, allowing ourselves to become positively wounded, and letting our hearts experience sad feelings, we are building resiliency and insulating ourselves from adversity that will come in the future. When you decide to redefine your grief, it will shift your reality.

There is so much value in befriending your pain. I hope this book will help you transform the negative association you may have with grief from an uncomfortable feeling you are used to avoiding to a new association of appreciation. You can find the magic in *your* tragic.

ART, MUSIC, AND DRAMA REFERENCES

PAINTINGS
>Hopper, Edward. *Nighthawks*. 1942.
>Magritte, René. *La Condition Humaine*. 1933.
>Magritte, René. *The Treachery of Images* ("This is not a pipe"). 1929.
>van Gogh, Vincent. *Wheatfield with Crows*. 1890.
>Wyeth, Andrew. *Christina's World*. 1948.

SCULPTURES
>György, Albert. *Melancholy*. 1987.

MUSIC
>Beethoven, Ludwig van. Piano Concerto No. 5, *Emperor*, Adagio. 1809.
>Chopin, Frédéric. Nocturne No. 21 in C Minor. 1837.
>Debussy, Claude. *Clair de Lune*. 1890.
>Dvořák, Antonín. Symphony No. 9, *New World*, Adagio. 1893.
>Flaming Lips. "Do You Realize?" 2002.
>Grieg, Edvard. Piano Concerto in A Minor, Op. 16., Adagio. 1868.

ART, MUSIC, AND DRAMA REFERENCES

Mahler, Gustav. Symphony No. 5, Adagio. 1901–1902.
Massenet, Jules. *Thaïs,* Act 2: Méditation (arr. for piano and cello). 1893.
Mozart, Wolfgang Amadeus. Piano Concerto No. 21, *Elvira Madigan.* 1785.
Ravel, Maurice. *Pavane pour une infante défunte.* 1899.
Saint-Saëns, Camille. *Le Cygne.* 1895.
Schumann, Robert. *Kinderszenen,* Op. 15, *Träumerie* (arr. for cello and orchestra). 1838.
The The. "Lonely Planet." 1993.
Wagner, Richard. *Tannhäuser,* Overture. 1845.

FILM AND TV
Amadeus. 1984.
Breaking Bad. 2008–2013.
Forrest Gump. 1994.
Frida. 2002.
Gunfight at the O.K. Corral. 1957.
Harold and Maude. 1971.
Lust for Life. 1956.
Pollock. 2000.
The Secret Life of Walter Mitty. 1947.
Titanic. 1997.

DRAMATICAL PLAYS
Shakespeare, William. *Hamlet.* 1599–1601.
Shakespeare, William. *The Merchant of Venice.* 1596–1598.
Sophocles, *Antigone.* 441 BC.

NOTES

INTRODUCTION
1. Victor Frankl, *Man's Search for Meaning* (Beacon Press, 1959; Ebury, 2013), Postscript.
2. Brad Stulberg, *Master of Change* (Heligo, 2023), 56–57.
3. Nassir Ghaemi, *A First-Rate Madness: Uncovering the Links Between Leadership and Mental Illness* (Penguin, 2011), 118.
4. Pema Chödrön, *The Places That Scare You* (Shambhala, 2010).
5. Chödrön, *Places That Scare You*, 9.
6. Maggie Jackson, "How to Thrive in an Uncertain World," *New York Times,* January 13, 2024, https://www.nytimes.com/2024/01/13/opinion/uncertainty-anxiety-psychology.html.
7. Susan Cain, *Bittersweet* (Penguin, 2022), 61.

CHAPTER 1: DISCOVERING THE DIGNITY IN SUFFERING
1. Eckhart Tolle, *Stillness Speaks* (New World Library, 2003), 126.
2. David Brooks, "How to Stay Sane in Brutalizing Times," *New York Times,* November 2, 2023, https://www.nytimes.com/2023/11/02/opinion/sunday/resilience-bad-news-coping.html.
3. "The Vocabularist: 'Tragedy' Originally Meant 'Goat-Song,'" *BBC News,* May 17, 2016, https://www.bbc.com/news/magazine-36276651.

NOTES

4. Aristotle, *Poetics*, trans. S. H. Butcher, MIT, The Internet Classics Archive, https://classics.mit.edu/Aristotle/poetics.1.1.html.
5. William Shakespeare, *Hamlet*, ed. Barbara A. Mowat and Paul Werstine (Washington Square Press, 2004), 3.2.70–71.
6. Kahlil Gibran, *The Prophet* (1923; Sterling, 2009), 32.
7. Wolfgang Amadeus Mozart, Piano Concerto No. 21 in C Major, K 467, *Elvira Madigan*.
8. Gibran, *The Prophet*, 16.
9. Catherine Kautsky, *Debussy's Paris: Piano Portraits of the Belle Epoque* (Rowman & Littlefield, 2017); Stephen Walsh, *Debussy: A Painter in Sound* (Knopf Doubleday, 2018).
10. Paul Verlaine, *Lumieres Sur Les Fetes Galantes*, "Clair de Lune" (1869; Librarie Nizet, 1959).
11. Claude Debussy, *Suite bergamasque*, mvt. 3, "Clair de Lune" (E. Fromont, 1905).
12. Chris Routledge, trans., "Featured Poem: Clair de Lune by Paul Verlaine," *The Reader*, March 30, 2009, https://www.thereader.org.uk/featured-poem-3/.
13. Cain, *Bittersweet*, xxi.
14. Nienke Bakker et al., *Vincent van Gogh: A Life in Letters* (Thames & Hudson, 2020); Jan Greenberg and Sandra Jordan, *Vincent van Gogh: Portrait of an Artist* (Yearling, 2003).
15. Rick Hanson, *Resilient: How to Grow an Unshakable Core of Calm, Strength, and Happiness* (Harmony, 2018), 9.
16. Vincent van Gogh, Museum Folkwang Essen, *Vincent van Gogh and the Modern Movement, 1890–1914*, ed. Georg W. Koltzsch (Luca, 1990), 186.
17. R. J. Anderson, *Ultraviolet* (Carolrhoda Lab, 2011), 291.
18. Neil deGrasse Tyson, *Starry Messenger* (Henry Holt and Company, 2022), 21.

CHAPTER 2: REAUTHORING OUR WOUNDS

1. John J. Prendergast, *The Deep Heart: Our Portal to Presence* (Sounds True, 2019), 28.

NOTES

2. Yehuda Halevi, "Tis a Fearful Thing," *Dīwān*, a collection of Hebrew poems written between the 1080s and 1141; first published in English in 1851.
3. Alice Miller, *The Drama of the Gifted Child: The Search for the True Self* (Basic Books, 1997).
4. Hillel Halkin, *Yehuda Halevi* (Schocken, 2010).
5. Jo Nash, PhD, "How to Accept the Impermanence of Life: A Buddhist Take," Positive Psychology, April 14, 2016, https://positivepsychology.com/impermanence/.
6. Pema Chödrön, *How We Live Is How We Die* (Shambhala, 2023), 79.
7. Museum of Modern Art, "Andrew Wyeth: *Christina's World*, 1948," accessed September 11, 2024, https://www.moma.org/collection/works/78455.
8. Richard Meryman, *Andrew Wyeth: A Secret Life* (Harper Perennial, 1998); Thomas Padon, *Andrew Wyeth: People and Places* (Rizzoli Electa, 2017).
9. Arthur C. Brooks, *From Strength to Strength* (Portfolio, 2022).
10. B. Raven Lee, *Unbinding the Soul* (pub. by author, 2015), 8.
11. Bonnie Kemske, *Kintsugi: The Poetic Mend* (Herbert Press, 2021).

CHAPTER 3: ACCESSING SPIRITUAL WELL-BEING

1. Brad Stulberg, *The Master of Change* (HarperOne, 2023), 170.
2. William Shakespeare, *The Merchant of Venice*, Barbara Mowat, Paul Werstine, et al., eds. (Folger Shakespeare Library, n.d.), accessed September 11, 2024, https://www.folger.edu/explore/shakespeares-works/the-merchant-of-venice/read/, 5.1.85—86.
3. Rick Hanson, *Resilient: How to Grow an Unshakable Core of Calm, Strength, and Happiness* (Harmony, 2018), 97.
4. Britannica Editors, "Heraclitus," *Encyclopedia Britannica*, August 23, 2024, https://www.britannica.com/biography/Heraclitus.
5. Camelia E. Hostinar, "Recent Developments in the Study of Social Relationships, Stress, Responses, and Physical Health,"

NOTES

Current Opinions in Psychology 5 (2015): 90–95, https://www.ncbi.nlm.nih.gov/pmc/articles/PMC4562328/.
6. Hostinar, "Recent Developments."
7. Héctor García and Francesc Miralles, *Ikigai: The Japanese Secret to a Long and Happy Life* (Penguin Life, 2017), 40.

CHAPTER 4: HEALTHY ALONENESS

1. John Leland, "How Loneliness Is Damaging Our Health," *New York Times*, April 20, 2022, https://www.nytimes.com/2022/04/20/nyregion/loneliness-epidemic.html.
2. Ashley Abramson, "Substance Use During the Pandemic," American Psychiatric Association, March 1, 2021, https://www.apa.org/monitor/2021/03/substance-use-pandemic.
3. Amy Novotney, "The Risks of Social Isolation," American Psychological Association, May 2019, https://www.apa.org/monitor/2019/05/ce-corner-isolation..
4. Leland, "How Loneliness Is Damaging Our Health."
5. Justin Spring, *The Essential Edward Hopper* (Barnes & Noble, 2007); Gail Levin, *Edward Hopper: An Intimate Biography* (University of California Press, 2023).
6. James Peacock, "Edward Hopper: The Artist Who Evoked Urban Loneliness and Disappointment with Beautiful Clarity," The Conversation, Yahoo News, updated May 18, 2017, https://uk.news.yahoo.com/edward-hopper-artist-evoked-urban-100158470.html?guccounter=1.
7. Olivia Laing, *The Lonely City: Adventures in the Art of Being Alone* (Picador, 2017), 44.
8. Sheryl Sandberg, "When tragedy occurs . . .," Facebook, June 3, 2015, https://www.facebook.com/photo.php?fbid=10155617891025177&set=a.404308695176.365039.717545176&type=1&theater.

NOTES

CHAPTER 5: FINDING THE OPTIMISM IN DEPRESSION

1. Kirsten Weir, "New Paths for People with Prolonged Grief Disorder," American Psychological Association, November 2018, https://www.apa.org/monitor/2018/11/ce-corner.
2. APA, "Prolonged Grief Disorder," American Psychiatric Association, accessed September 11, 2024, https://www.psychiatry.org/patients-families/prolonged-grief-disorder.
3. APA, "Prolonged Grief Disorder."
4. Chinenye Onyemaechi, MD, "Depression," American Psychological Association, accessed September 11, 2024, https://www.psychiatry.org/patients-families/depression.
5. NIH, "Any Anxiety Disorder," National Institute of Mental Health, accessed September 1, 2024, https://www.nimh.nih.gov/health/statistics/any-anxiety-disorder; NIH, "Major Depression," National Institute of Mental Health, accessed September 2, 2024, https://www.nimh.nih.gov/health/statistics/major-depression.
6. Dan Witters, "U.S. Depression Rates Reach New Highs," Gallup, May 17, 2023, https://news.gallup.com/poll/505745/depression-rates-reach-new-highs.aspx.
7. Arthur J. Davidson et al., "Monitoring Depression Rates in an Urban Community: Use of Electronic Health Records," *Journal of Public Health Management and Practice* 24, no. 6 (2018): E6–E14, https://www.ncbi.nlm.nih.gov/pmc/articles/PMC6170150/.
8. Joshua Wolf Shenk, "Lincoln's Great Depression," *Atlantic*, October 2005, https://www.theatlantic.com/magazine/archive/2005/10/lincolns-great-depression/304247/.
9. John Banks, "Abraham Lincoln's Family: Meet the Key Members," February 12, 2024, https://www.history.com/news/abraham-lincoln-family.
10. Claudia Kalb, *Andy Warhol Was a Hoarder* (National Geographic Society, 2016), 115.
11. Kalb, *Andy Warhol*.

NOTES

12. Nassir Ghaemi, *A First-Rate Madness: Uncovering the Links Between Leadership and Mental Illness* (Penguin, 2012), 57.
13. Ghaemi, 90.
14. Quoted in Richard Attenborough, *Gandhi: In My Own Words* (Hodder and Stoughton, 2002), 3.
15. Quoted in Keith D. Miller, *Voice of Deliverance: The Language of Martin Luther King* (University of Georgia Press, 1998), 107.
16. John Sturges, dir., *Gunfight at the O.K. Corral* (Hal Wallis, 1957).

CHAPTER 6: WHY WE WORRY

1. Jennifer N. Morey et al., "Current Directions in Stress and Human Immune Function," *Current Opinions in Psychology* 5 (October 2015): 13–17, https://www.ncbi.nlm.nih.gov/pmc/articles/PMC4465119/.
2. Daniel Collerton, "Psychotherapy and Brain Plasticity," *Frontiers in Psychology* 4 (2013): 548, https://www.ncbi.nlm.nih.gov/pmc/articles/PMC3764373/.
3. Adam Grant, *Hidden Potential* (Ebury, 2023), 68.
4. Todd Alden, *The Essential René Magritte* (Wonderland Press, 1999), 24.
5. Susan Cain, *Bittersweet* (Crown, 2022), 19.
6. Claudia Kalb, *Andy Warhol Was a Hoarder* (National Geographic Society, 2018).
7. Kalb, *Andy Warhol*, 199.
8. Charles Darwin, *The Beagle Letters,* ed. Frederick Burkhardt (Cambridge University Press, 2008).
9. Darwin, *The Beagle Letters,* 76.

CHAPTER 7: THE MYTH OF CLOSURE

1. Marisa Renee Lee, *Grief Is Love: Living with Loss* (Hachette, 2022), 47.
2. Ella Wheeler Wilcox, "Solitude," *Poems of Passion* (1883), Poetry Foundation, https://www.poetryfoundation.org/poems/45937/solitude-56d225aad9924.

NOTES

3. JongEun Yim, "Therapeutic Benefits of Laughter in Mental Health: A Theoretical Review," *Tohoku Journal of Experimental Medicine* 239, no. 3 (2016): 243–49, https://doi.org/10.1620/tjem.239.243.
4. Ashley Marcin, "9 Ways Crying May Benefit Your Health," Healthline, April 14, 2017, https://www.healthline.com/health/benefits-of-crying.
5. "Psychologist: Grief Is Shock, Then Anger," CNN, March 24, 2014, accessed April 7, 2014, https://www.cnn.com/videos/world/2014/03/24/ctw-psychologist-on-malaysia-flight-370-families.cnn.
6. Anderson Cooper, "Counselor: No Closure for MH370 Families," CNN, March 20, 2014, accessed September 13, 2024, https://edition.cnn.com/videos/world/2014/03/20/ac-intv-yin-grief-counselor-flight-370-families.cnn.
7. Elisabeth Kübler-Ross, *On Death and Dying* (Simon & Schuster, 1970).
8. Kübler-Ross, *On Death*.
9. Gary Greenberg, "In Grief Is How We Live Now," *New York Times*, May 7, 2022, https://www.nytimes.com/2022/05/07/opinion/grief.html.
10. Marcel Proust, *Time Regained* (1926), in Susan Ratcliffe, ed., *Oxford Essential Quotations* (Oxford University Press, 2018), https://www.oxfordreference.com/display/10.1093/acref/9780191866692.001.0001/q-oro-ed6-00008648.
11. Romina Godoy, "Melancholy," Where Creativity Works, April 7, 2021, https://wherecreativityworks.com/melancholy/.
12. Henry Wadsworth Longfellow, *Longfellow's Hyperion, Kavanagh, and The Trouveres,* ed. Ernest Rhys (Camelot Classics, 1887), 51.
13. Érika Arantes de Oliveira Cardoso et al., "The Effect of Suppressing Funeral Rituals During the COVID-19 Pandemic on Bereaved Families," *Revista Latino-Americana de Enfermagem*, National Library of Medicine, vol. 28, September 7, 2020, https://www.ncbi.nlm.nih.gov/pmc/articles/PMC7478881/.

14. Eduardo Medina, "Mourning Families Seek Solace from the 'Grief Purgatory' of Covid-19," *New York Times,* July 31, 2021, https://www.nytimes.com/2021/07/31/us/coronavirus-grief-funerals.html.
15. Sophocles, *Antigone,* trans. Reginald Gibbons and Charles Segal (Oxford University Press, 2007).
16. Sophocles, *Antigone.*
17. Sophocles, *Antigone.*

CHAPTER 8: MINDFULNESS

1. Mindful Staff, "Jon Kabat-Zinn: Defining Mindfulness," Mindful, January 11, 2017, https://www.mindful.org/jon-kabat-zinn-defining-mindfulness/#:~:text=Mindfulness%20is%20awareness%20that%20arises,%2C%E2%80%9D%20says%20Kabat%2DZinn.
2. Eckhart Tolle, "Acceptance of the Seemingly Unacceptable," YouTube, uploaded by PLOTOON LTD, September 26, 2023, released January 1, 2022, https://www.youtube.com/watch?v=yD6T66zs-8c.
3. Bhante Henepola Gunaratana, *Mindfulness in Plain English* (Wisdom, 2011), 135.
4. Bo Forbes, *Yoga for Emotional Balance* (Shambhala, 2011), 8.
5. Forbes, *Yoga,* 37.
6. Deepak Chopra, *The Seven Spiritual Laws of Success* (Amber-Allen, 1994), 86.
7. Pema Chödrön, *Comfortable with Uncertainty: 108 Teachings on Cultivating Fearlessness and Compassion* (Shambhala, 2002), 109.

CHAPTER 9: THE POWER OF SELF-REGULATION

1. Todd F. Heatherton and Dylan D. Wagner, "Cognitive Neuroscience of Self-Regulation Failure," *Trends in Cognitive Science* 15, no. 3 (March 2011): 132–39, https://www.ncbi.nlm.nih.gov/pmc/articles/PMC3062191/; J. F. Banfield et al., "The Cognitive Neuroscience of Self-Regulation," in R. F. Baumeister

and K. D. Vohs, eds., *Handbook of Self-Regulation: Research, Theory, and Applications* (Guilford, 2004), 62–83, https://psycnet.apa.org/record/2004-00163-003; Todd F. Heatherton, "Neuroscience of Self and Self-Regulation," *Annual Review of Psychology* 62 (2011): 363–90, https://www.ncbi.nlm.nih.gov/pmc/articles/PMC3056504/; Deleene S. Menefee et al., "The Importance of Regulation in Mental Health," *American Journal of Lifestyle Medicine* 16, no. 1 (2022): 28–31, https://www.ncbi.nlm.nih.gov/pmc/articles/PMC8848120/.
2. Matthew J. Girgenti et al., "Molecular and Cellular Effects of Traumatic Stress: Implications for PTSD," *Current Psychiatry Reports* 19, no. 11 (2017): 85, https://www.ncbi.nlm.nih.gov/pmc/articles/PMC5907804/.
3. Bessel van der Kolk, *The Body Keeps the Score* (Penguin, 2015), 62, 63, 82.
4. Maureen McCarthy Draper, *The Nature of Music: Beauty, Sound, and Healing* (Riverhead Books, 2001).
5. Cyrus Darki et al., "The Effect of Classical Music on Heart Rate, Blood Pressure, and Mood," *Cureus* 14, no. 7 (July 2022), https://www.ncbi.nlm.nih.gov/pmc/articles/PMC9417331/.
6. Laura Ferreri et al., "Dopamine Modulates the Reward Experiences Elicited by Music," *Proceedings of the National Academy of Sciences* 116, no. 9 (February 2019): 3793–3798, https://www.ncbi.nlm.nih.gov/pmc/articles/PMC6397525/.
7. Norman Lebrecht, *Why Beethoven: A Phenomenon in One Hundred Pieces* (Pegasus, 2023), 33.
8. Martin Cooper, *Beethoven: The Last Decade 1817–1827* (Oxford University Press, 1970).

CHAPTER 10: THE NEED FOR NOSTALGIA

1. Catherine Caruso, "What Happens in the Brain While Daydreaming?" *Harvard Gazette,* December 13, 2023, https://news.harvard.edu/gazette/story/2023/12/researchers-one-step-closer-to-understanding-daydreams/; Jiangzhou Sun

NOTES

et al., "The Bright Side and Dark Side of Daydreaming: Predict Creativity Together Through Brain Functional Connectivity," *Human Brain Mapping* 43, no. 3 (February 15, 2022): 902–14, https://www.ncbi.nlm.nih.gov/pmc/articles/PMC8764487/; Monica C. Parker, "Why Daydreaming Is So Good for You," *Time,* February 21, 2023, https://time.com/6256541/why-daydreaming-is-good-for-you/; Rebecca L. McMillan et al., "Ode to Positive Constructive Daydreaming," *Frontiers in Psychology* 4 (2013): 626, https://www.ncbi.nlm.nih.gov/pmc/articles/PMC3779797/.

2. Kate Murphy, "Pandemic-Proof Your Habits," *New York Times,* November 8, 2020, https://www.nytimes.com/2020/11/28/sunday-review/pandemic-habits-routine-brain.html.
3. Phil G. Goulding, *Classical Music: 50 Great Composers and Their 1,000 Greatest Works* (Random House, 1995), 191.
4. Goulding, *Classical Music,* 140.

CHAPTER 11: THE IMPORTANCE OF EMOTIONAL VULNERABILITY

1. Alissa Quart, "Can We Put an End to America's Most Dangerous Myth?" *New York Times,* March 9, 2023, https://www.nytimes.com/2023/03/09/opinion/art-of-dependence.html.
2. Arthur Schopenhauer, *Essays and Aphorisms,* trans. R. J. Hollingdale (Penguin Classics, 1970), 50.
3. Schopenhauer, *Essays.*
4. Alan Watts, "The Age of Insecurity," in *The Wisdom of Insecurity* (1951; Ebury, 2012), 13.
5. Brené Brown, *Daring Greatly* (Avery, 2015).
6. Beth Kempton, *Wabi Sabi: Japanese Wisdom for a Perfectly Imperfect Life* (Little, Brown, 2018), 95.
7. Ellen Hendriksen, *How to Be Yourself* (St. Martin's, 2018), 75–76.
8. Hendriksen, *How to Be Yourself,* 75.
9. Hendriksen, *How to Be Yourself,* 75–76.
10. John Bradshaw, *Healing the Shame that Binds You* (Health Communications, 1988).

NOTES

11. David A. Fryburg, "Kindness as a Stress Reduction-Health Promotion Intervention: A Review of the Psychobiology of Caring," *American Journal of Lifestyle Medicine* 16, no. 1 (2022): 89–100, https://www.ncbi.nlm.nih.gov/pmc/articles/PMC8848115/.
12. Rick Hanson, *Resilient* (Harmony, 2018), 14.
13. Kristin Neff, *Self-Compassion: The Proven Power of Being Yourself* (Hodder & Stoughton, 2011), 110.
14. "Lonely Planet," by Matt Johnson, track 10 on The The, *Dusk*, Sony, 1993.
15. Hanson, *Resilient,* 21.

CHAPTER 12: LEARNING TO LIVE LIKE THE OCEAN

1. Leonard Cohen, "Good Advice for Someone Like Me," Leonard Cohen Files, accessed October 10, 2024, https://leonardcohenfiles.com/goodadvice.html.
2. Henry Douglas Wild, *Shakespeare, Prophet for Our Time* (Theosophical Publishing House, 1972), 63.
3. William Shakespeare, *Hamlet,* Barbara Mowat et al., eds., Folger Shakespeare Library, accessed September 19, 2024, Act 1, Scene 5, lines 759–761, https://www.folger.edu/explore/shakespeares-works/hamlet/read/1/5/.
4. Shakespeare, *Hamlet,* 3.1.64.
5. Shakespeare, *Hamlet,* 3.1.66–67.
6. Robert Zemeckis, dir., *Forrest Gump* (Paramount Pictures, 1994).
7. Aldous Huxley, *Texts and Pretexts* (Harper & Brothers, 1933), 5.
8. Patrick Olivelle, "Karma," *Encyclopedia Britannica*, accessed September 19, 2024, https://www.britannica.com/topic/karma.
9. Shakespeare, *Hamlet,* 3.1.67.
10. Hal Ashby, dir., *Harold and Maude* (Paramount Pictures, 1971).
11. Neil Pasricha, *The Book of Awesome* (G. P. Putnam's Sons, 2011), 167, 264.

BIBLIOGRAPHY

Alden, Todd. *The Essential René Magritte*. Wonderland, 1999.
American Psychiatric Association. *Diagnostic and Statistical Manual of Mental Disorders: DSM-5 TR*. American Psychiatric Association Publishing, 2022.
Aurelius, Marcus. *Meditations*. Penguin, 2006.
Bakker, Nienke. *Vincent Van Gogh: A Life in Letters*. Thames and Hudson Limited, 2021.
Baumgartner, Karen and Thomas Padon. *Andrew Wyeth: People and Places*. Rizzoli Electa, 2017.
Bradshaw, John. *Healing the Shame that Binds You*. Health Communications, 1988.
Brooks, Arthur C. *From Strength to Strength*. Portfolio Penguin, 2022.
Brooks, Arthur C. and Oprah Winfrey. *Build the Life You Want*. Ebury, 2023.
Brown, Brené. *Daring Greatly*. Avery, 2012.
Brown, Brené. *The Gifts of Imperfection*. Hazelden, 2010.
Cain, Susan. *Bittersweet*. Crown, 2022.
Cain, Susan. *Quiet*. Crown, 2012.
Chödrön, Pema. *How We Live Is How We Die*. Shambhala, 2023.
Chödrön, Pema. *The Places That Scare You*. Shambhala, 2002.
Chopra, Deepak. *The Seven Spiritual Laws of Success*. Amber-Allen, 1994.

BIBLIOGRAPHY

Cohen, Leonard. *The Flame: Poems, Notebooks, Lyrics, Drawings.* Farrar, Straus and Giroux, 2018.
Draper, Maureen McCarthy. *The Nature of Music: Beauty, Sound and Healing.* Penguin, 2001.
Egan, Gerard. *Face to Face.* Brooks/Cole, 2007.
Farnsworth, Ward. *The Practicing Stoic.* David R. Godine, 2018.
Forbes, Bo. *Yoga for Emotional Balance.* Shambhala, 2011.
Frankl, Viktor E. *Man's Search for Meaning.* Ebury, 2013.
García, Héctor and Francesc Miralles. *Ikigai: The Japanese Secret to a Long and Happy Life.* Penguin Life, 2017.
Ghaemi, Nassir. *A First-Rate Madness: Uncovering the Links Between Leadership and Mental Illness.* Penguin, 2011.
Gibran, Kahlil. *The Prophet.* University of California, Berkeley, 1923; Sterling, 2009.
Gladwell, Malcolm. *Blink.* Penguin, 2006.
Goulding, Phil G. *Classical Music: The 50 Greatest Composers and Their 1,000 Greatest Works.* Random House, 1995.
Grant, Adam. *Hidden Potential.* Ebury, 2023.
Grant, Adam. *Originals.* Penguin, 2016.
Grant, Adam. *Think Again.* Ebury, 2021.
Greenberg, Gary. *The Book of Woe: The DSM and the Unmaking of Psychiatry.* Penguin, 2013.
Greenberg, Jan. *Vincent van Gogh, Portrait of an Artist.* Yearling, 2003.
Gunaratana, Bhante Henepola. *Mindfulness in Plain English.* Wisdom, 2011.
Halkin, Hillel. *Yehuda Halevi.* Schocken, 2010.
Hanh, Thich Nhat. *No Death, No Fear.* Ebury, 2012.
Hanson, Rick. *Resilient.* Harmony, 2018.
Hendriksen, Ellen. *How to Be Yourself.* St. Martin's, 2018.
Holiday, Ryan. *The Obstacle Is the Way.* Penguin, 2014.
Huxley, Aldous. *The Doors of Perception.* Random House, 2010.
Jung, Carl. *The Undiscovered Self.* Princeton University Press, 2011.
Kabat-Zinn, Jon. *Letting Everything Become Your Teacher.* Random House, 2010.

BIBLIOGRAPHY

Kabat-Zinn, Jon. *Wherever You Go, There You Are*. Hachette, 2023.

Kalb, Claudia. *Andy Warhol Was a Hoarder*. National Geographic Society, 2018.

Kautsky, Catherine. *Debussy's Paris*. Rowman & Littlefield, 2017.

Kempton, Beth. *Wabi Sabi: Japanese Wisdom for a Perfectly Imperfect Life*. Little, Brown, 2018.

Kemske, Bonnie. *Kintsugi: The Poetic Mend*. Bloomsbury, 2021.

Kübler-Ross, Elizabeth. *On Death and Dying*. Simon & Schuster, 1970.

Laing, Olivia. *The Lonely City: Adventures in the Art of Being Alone*. Picador, 2017.

Lebrecht, Norman. *Why Beethoven: A Phenomenon in One Hundred Pieces*. Pegasus, 2023.

Lee, B. Raven. *Unbinding the Soul*. Published by the author, 2015.

Lee, Marisa Renee. *Grief Is Love*. Grand Central, 2022.

Levin, Gail. *Edward Hopper: An Intimate Biography*. University of California Press, 2023.

Meryman, Richard. *Andrew Wyeth: A Secret Life*. Harper Perennial, 1998.

Miller, Alice. *The Drama of the Gifted Child*. Basic Books, 1997.

Miller, Alice. *Thou Shalt Not Be Aware*. Farrar, Straus, and Giroux, 1998.

Neff, Kristin. *Self-Compassion: The Proven Power of Being Yourself*. Hodder & Stoughton, 2011.

Pasricha, Neil. *The Book of Awesome*. G. P. Putnam's Sons, 2010.

Quart, Alissa. *Bootstrapped: Liberating Ourselves from the American Dream*. HarperCollins, 2023.

Rando, Therese A. *How to Go on Living When Someone You Love Dies*. Echo Point, 2023.

Roche, Paul, trans. *Sophocles: The Complete Plays*. Signet Classics, 2010.

Rosenzweig, Franz. *Ninety-Two Poems and Hymns of Yehuda Halevi*. State University of New York Press, 2012.

Rough Guides. *A Rough Guide to Classical Music*, 4th ed. Rough Guides, 2005.

BIBLIOGRAPHY

Sartre, Jean Paul. *Existentialism Is a Humanism*. Yale University Press, 2007.

Schopenhauer, Arthur. *Essays and Aphorisms*. Penguin Classics, 1970.

Schopenhauer, Arthur. *Parerga and Parlipomena*, Volume 2. Cambridge University Press, 2014.

Schopenhauer, Arthur. *The Wisdom of Life*. S. Sonnenschein & Company, 1891.

Seneca, Lucius. *Letters from a Stoic*. Penguin, 2004.

Sharma, Robin. *The 5 AM Club*. HarperCollins, 2018.

Shenk, Joshua Wolf. *Lincoln's Melancholy*. Houghton Mifflin, 2006.

Simmons, Sylvie. *I'm Your Man: The Life of Leonard Cohen*. Random House, 2012.

Spring, Justin. *The Essential Edward Hopper*. Barnes & Noble, 2007.

Storr, Francis, trans. *Sophocles: The Three Theban Plays*. Digireads, 2016.

Stulberg, Brad. *Master of Change*. HarperCollins, 2023.

Tolle, Eckhart. *A New Earth*. Penguin, 2006.

Tolle, Eckhart. *Stillness Speaks*. New World Library, 2003.

Tolle, Eckhart. *The Power of Now*. Namaste, 2004.

Tsilimparis, John. *Retrain Your Anxious Brain*. Harlequin, 2014.

Tyson, Neil deGrasse. *Starry Messenger: Cosmic Perspectives on Civilization*. Henry Holt and Company, 2022.

van der Kolk, Bessel. *The Body Keeps the Score*. Penguin, 2015.

W., Bill. *Alcoholics Anonymous: The Big Book*. Dover, 2019.

Walsh, Stephen. *Debussy: A Painter in Sound*. Knopf Doubleday, 2018.

Watts, Alan W. *The Wisdom of Insecurity*. Ebury, 2012.

Wild, Henry Douglas. *Shakespeare: Prophet for Our Time*. Theosophical Publishing House, 1971.

Yalom, Irvin. *Staring at the Sun*. Wiley, 2010.

Zabus, Vincent. *Magritte: This Is Not a Biography*. Harry N. Abrams, 2017.

ACKNOWLEDGMENTS

MY LATE FATHER, SPYROS ARISTEDES TSILIMPARIS, WAS NOT A man who expressed his love through words. He instead expressed it by sharing his passion for the arts and humanities. He enjoyed educating people with his deep knowledge of artistic culture, history, and philosophy and his infatuation with beauty. He was at his happiest when he had a captive audience. To many people, my father was a spiritual guru, sage, and mystic. He claimed that his sole purpose for living was "to inspire and to be inspired."

Most of the classical and artistic references featured in this book were passed on to me by my father. I am eternally grateful for that gift. His heart and soul are embodied in every chapter. *The Magic in the Tragic* is an elegy to his memory.

There are many other people to acknowledge for this journey. It doesn't necessarily take a village, but getting a book developed, edited, and published is definitely a team sport.

The dream team: My intrepid editor and star quarterback, Kara Mannix, at Harper Celebrate. Without her leadership and strategic play-calling, *The Magic in the Tragic* would never

ACKNOWLEDGMENTS

have been completed. I am grateful for her shared vision and unlimited patience. Thanks to my two other wise and indispensable editors: Bonnie Honeycutt and Jenn McNeil.

Thanks to Michael Aulisio, VP/Publisher at HarperCollins, and Robin Richardson-Houston. Thanks to my literary agent, Linda Konner, who believed in the value of this book from the very beginning.

Heartfelt thanks to my family, who encourage me to remember who I am: My mother, Rosario Hernandez Tsilimparis, the kindest person I've ever known; my brother, Adonis Tsilimparis, and his wife, Dena Boykins; Blanca Millan; Manny Millan; Sister Carla Hernandez; Alexis Ford Hernandez.

To my steadfast friends (blood makes you related, but loyalty makes you family): Christian S. Alexander, Arlene Saryan, Patricia Bell Palmer, Isaac Palmer, Clifford M. Shikler, Christina Mansfield Ross, Karen Pickett, Deborah Carmichael, Deborah Winer, Cindy Levinson, Michael Ladd, Julia Ladd, Chaille DeFaria, John DeFaria.

An enthusiastic shout-out to other individuals who have positively influenced the contents of this book: literary editor Dave Groff, Dr. Claire Ciliotta, Dr. Jennifer Langham, Dr. Amir Ettekal, Jim Carter, Kathleen Gray, Tony Cookson, Kim Cookson, Andrea Rogers, Cecile Munoz, Juan Fernandez, Shawn Meaux, Roger Steele, Lysa Barry, Ellen Leyva, Marla Tellez, Ekkehard Piening, Mariana Bomfim Magness.

And to the founders and fellow advisory board members of Wondermind (Wondermind.com), the world's first mental

ACKNOWLEDGMENTS

health fitness ecosystem, thanks for allowing me to be part of a great organization.

Lastly, I am indebted to the many artists, composers, and writers whose creative expressions give me the strength to embrace my grief rather than fear it. They teach me how to aesthetically reframe hardship with game-changing optimism.

One of the most important skills we can acquire in this life is to embrace the totality of being human. Holding suffering close to my heart helps me remember how to live. Adversity is my existential fuel.

JOHN TSILIMPARIS, MFT, IS A DISTINGUISHED PSYCHOTHERAPIST, mental health consultant, podcast host, and former adjunct professor at Pepperdine University and UCLA Extension. He's the author of *Retrain Your Anxious Brain* (Hanover Square Press, 2022).

John is a former staff therapist in the department of psychiatry at Cedars-Sinai Medical Center and in the department of addiction medicine at Kaiser Permanente. He's a member of the Advisory Board Committee for the popular and prestigious mental health platform Wondermind (Wondermind.com).

In his private practice, John focuses on treating individuals suffering from depression, grief and loss, severe anxiety disorders like OCD, phobias, panic disorder, and trauma. He also treats couples and families.

John is a lover of the arts and the curative allure that creativity inspires. He is also a musician and a published composer. He lives in Los Angeles, California.